Contents

Acknowledgements

The initial idea for this work emerged from earlier work on local authority assessment practice which was undertaken by two of us and published as *Squaring the circle* (Ellis, 1993a). Our idea for researching access to assessment took shape in discussions with Averil Osborne. It became a research proposal just before Averil's death in July 1994. We learnt a great deal through her thoughtful guidance and committed concern.

We would like to thank Barbara Webb for her work in seeing us and the Advisory Group through the initial phase of our research and Claire Benjamin who steered us through the middle and final phases.

We would also like to acknowledge the way in which the Joseph Rowntree Foundation responded positively to the project's development and extended financial help to ensure that the project would have a direct relevance to those disabled people and carers who are negotiating local authority assessments.

This research project and report has been completed because of the support and commitment of many people. Our thanks go to the practitioners and managers of the two social services departments, and the voluntary organisation. They welcomed us, gave us access to their documents and data and allowed us to observe their practice. We thank them too for their tolerant and perceptive responses to our feedback. We would also like to thank the users and carers groups who gave us time, direction, advice and information as we discovered the local terrain in which assessment work was being undertaken.

Central to the completion of the project were the 73 people who responded so positively to our requests for interviews. Welcoming us into their homes and lives and generously giving attention to our concerns, they shared their experiences of assessment, as well as their ideas for positive change. We are indebted to all of them.

In completing the interviews we were helped by Rosemary Littlechild who provided interviewing advice and Usha Mehta who acted as interpreter. Our thanks to them and to the British Sign Language interpreters who assisted us with the interviews with Deaf people.

Throughout this project we were able to draw on the expertise and support of two groups who gave dedicated time to the project. The Project Advisory group of Charlie Barker, Gill Crosse, Bob Findlay, Sarah Head, Noel Parry, Julia Twigg and Terry Vincent and the panel of disabled people and advisors, Judy Aspinall, Trevor Bailey, Stephen Daw, David Heap, Lesley Kelly, Edward Murtagh, Heather Patterson, Lorna Shaw, Tracey Shervington, Derek Vizor and Ruth Whapples, who worked with us and Simon Lippmann on a survival guide for disabled people on accessing assessment. We thank you all for your interest, energy and ideas.

Thanks are also due to Caroline Glendinning whose understanding and flexibility when one of us moved posts ensured the continuity of the project; Ann Lane who worked skilfully and tolerantly on the ebbs and flows of transcription in the midst of a busy office; and Sue Gilbert who prepared this manuscript.

In acknowledging our indebtedness to all those who have helped us make sense of access to community care assessments in the present climate, we recognise that the report may make uncomfortable reading at times. We have adopted a critical perspective on the dilemmas faced by organisations and practitioners working with new assessment arrangements in the hope that it will provide a stimulus for debate and change.

The companion to this report, *Community care assessments: what they are and how to get one*, is to be published by the Birmingham Disability Resource Centre in partnership with The University of Birmingham Department of Social Policy and Social Work, early in 1998.

Introduction

This study is concerned with how disabled people and carers are accessing local authority assessments for community care services. The research was undertaken in 1995 and 1996. It began two years after the full implementation of the 1990 National Health Service and Community Care Act (NHSCCA) which brought changes to the way in which local authority community care services were purchased and provided.

In the run up to full implementation of the NHSCCA in April 1993 the government issued volumes of guidance to local authority social services departments. This guidance emphasised the importance of assessment in the changes being made to the delivery of community care services. Assessment was described as 'the cornerstone' of good quality community care (DoH, 1990). It was argued that it was through assessment that disabled people could be brought closer to purchasing decisions. This would facilitate consumer empowerment and individualised, flexible responses to need (DoH, 1990; DoH et al, 1991a; 1991b; Audit Commission, 1992a; 1992b).

Our study explored how social work practitioners were using the new forms of assessment procedures which had been introduced by local authorities. It also asked disabled people and carers what they thought of these new arrangements for assessment. Through our research we observed the ways in which social workers were going about the business of assessing disabled people. We also sought the views of disabled people and carers about their assessment encounters with local authority social workers. In undertaking this research we observed the assessment practice of six social work teams in two local authorities. We also interviewed 50 disabled people and 23 carers who had had contact with these teams.

Chapter 1 sets the scene for the study. It considers the ways in which central government and local authority social services departments have viewed access to assessment. It outlines the approach promoted in guidance for assessing the needs of disabled people and carers, and the challenges it has posed for traditional social work assessment practice.

In **Chapter 2** we describe and analyse the range of ways in which social workers in the six teams of the two local authorities we researched were working with access to assessment. **Chapter 3** examines the assessment experiences which disabled people and carers shared with us, as well as the views they had about how practice could be improved. In the **Chapter 4** we consider the relevance of this study's findings for those currently working to improve assessment access and outcomes in local authority community care services.

We had three main interests in designing and undertaking this study. We wanted to increase understanding of the barriers faced by disabled people in accessing support and assistance to live full and independent lives. We were also concerned to explore how carers viewed assessment and were viewed as key informants by social workers undertaking assessments. Finally, our work sought to identify the ways in which disabled people and carers could, if they wished, play an active part in the arrangements which were being made to assess them for services.

This study offers testimony to the considerable difficulties facing disabled people and their households in accessing assessment for community care services. It also offers some ideas about how to increase the influence which disabled people have over developing more relevant and responsive assessment approaches.

Throughout the two years of this study we worked as researchers with a panel of disabled people who were members of a range of national organisations of disabled people. They brought their experience and expertise to our research design, delivery and dissemination.

As a response to sharing early analysis of our findings, the panel identified and researched the need for a guide, written for disabled people, about accessing assessment. The outcome of this work is the guide *Community care assessments: what they are and how to get one* published by Birmingham Disability Resource Centre and The University of Birmingham Department of Social Policy and Social Work (1998). As a companion volume to this report it provides information and support to disabled people seeking to live full and independent lives.

1
Setting the scene

When older and disabled people find that they need support and assistance, local authority social services departments are a potential resource on which they can call. Since full implementation of the 1990 National Health Service and Community Care Act (NHSCCA) social services departments have been given lead responsibility by central government in determining the kind of assistance that might be required and organising an appropriate response.

The impetus for government to introduce new arrangements for the delivery of community care was a concern to control social security spending on residential care (Lewis and Glennerster, 1996). Removing the perverse incentive favouring residential over community-based care would bring this spiralling budget under control and achieve the key government objective of securing 'better value for taxpayers' money' (DoH, 1990, para 1.1).

At the time of full implementation of the NHSCCA, official guidance also stated that "the rationale for this reorganisation is the empowerment of users and carers" (DoH et al, 1991a, p 9). Under the changed role of local authority social services departments, as purchasers rather than providers of services, assessment and care management systems would serve as gateways into the new mixed economy of care. People requiring assistance would be empowered by their greater proximity to purchasing decisions and their participation in the design of individualised, flexible responses to need.

Central to the success of these key objectives for community care was "to make proper assessment of need and good care management the cornerstone of high quality care" (DoH, 1990, para 1.1). The promotion of 'proper assessment of need' in new arrangements meant that assessment was destined to play a central part in resolving inherent tensions in policy aims that were several and conflicting.

The rest of this chapter examines the influence of these contradictory objectives on the design of assessment and care management systems, the role of front-line social worker practitioners, and the implications of policy ambiguity for the access of disabled people and carers to an assessment of need.

From service-led to needs-led assessments?

New arrangements for assessment and care management were heralded as promoting needs-led assessments. In its White Paper Caring for people, the government stated that "the objective of assessment is to determine the best available way to help the individual.... Assessment should not focus only on the user's suitability for a particular existing service" (Secretaries of State, 1989, para 3.2.3).

At the same time, assessment and care management systems had a key role to play in managing competing policy aims. They had to ensure both the most effective and efficient use of limited resources, and the full involvement of users and carers in the identification and assessment of their needs. Needs-led assessments were presented in policy guidance as a means of satisfying both objectives (DoH, 1990, ch 3):

- they improve disabled people's quality of life, by ensuring that they receive the support they need, rather than existing services which may not be right for them;

- they improve the cost-effectiveness of services, by ensuring that money is not wasted providing services that disabled people do not need.

Yet how was need to be defined? The Audit Commission advised local authorities to avoid creating unmeetable demand for services by linking their definition of need to the availability of resources. This, in turn, meant that "the definition of 'need' depends on priorities" (Audit Commission, 1992a, p 31). Better value for taxpayers' money would also be secured by targeting resources on those in greatest need.

The relative priority of need was to be assessed according to eligibility criteria measuring levels of 'risk'. The people most likely to receive services under new arrangements were those perceived to be in danger because of the lack of - or apparent fragility of - personal support.

If needs identified during assessment were defined in terms of eligibility criteria, and such criteria through prioritising, determined access to services, it is difficult to see how the desired shift of emphasis towards needs-led assessments was to be achieved. Yet 'need' and service criteria merge in official guidance. The Social Services Inspectorate (SSI) described assessment and care management as a linear process in which judgements about 'need' are formed prior to, and separately from, decisions about any services to be provided (DoH et al, 1991a; 1991b). However, the same prioritisation criteria govern thinking at all stages. Therefore definitions of 'need' used in assessment are based circular fashion on decisions about services.

Accessing an assessment

The same principle governed access to assessment and care management systems. The NHSCCA placed a duty to assess on local authorities (1990 NHSCCA, s 47) but this was limited to those people who appeared to require the services they purchased or provided. The result, as the evidence of a recent study of the implementation of community care changes shows, is that local authorities tend only to assess people considered to be at risk (Lewis and Glennerster, 1996).

The SSI also encouraged local authority social services departments to instigate simple and efficient procedures for relating level and type of assessment response to level and nature of need presented (DoH et al, 1991a, p 47). Under the new arrangements some enquiries would fail to become official referrals at all; of those accepted for assessment, the expectation was that most would receive a 'simple' or 'direct' assessment. This would consist of either the provision of advice, including rerouting to another agency, or of an assessment by a home care organiser or occupational therapist, leading to the provision of a discrete and low level of service. Only a minority of people would access a 'comprehensive' assessment and 'package of care'.

The desired match would be achieved by basing decisions about access to assessment, and its most appropriate type and level, on predicted service outcomes rather than on uncovered 'need'. The SSI advised practitioners that "the assessment should be commensurate with the likely input of care resources or the likely saving on resources by enabling the individual to cope in other ways" (DoH et al, 1991a, p 48).

People assessed as at high risk, for example, would be eligible for a full or comprehensive assessment on the basis that they appeared to require an intensive level of services, up to and including residential care, and/or a wide range of services requiring multidisciplinary input.

It seemed likely, therefore, that during the initial stages of assessment and care management, greater emphasis would be placed on ensuring service requests satisfied eligibility criteria than on opening up a dialogue about need with disabled people.

Service charging

Official guidance also made it clear that service charging had a role to play in containing expenditure. Local authorities had the power to make such charges for domiciliary (ie, non residential) care services as they considered reasonable (Baldwin and Lunt, 1996).

So long as assessments were needs-led then decisions about the requirement for services would only be taken after an individual's needs had been established. Nor could services be withdrawn or withheld from an individual assessed as needing them but unable to afford the service charge. In theory, then, ability and willingness to pay service charges would not form part of the eligibility criteria used to access an assessment for community care. Nor would means-testing begin until it had been established that an individual required a service.

The difficulty would arise where assessments of 'need' were effectively tests of eligibility for services. Then, it seemed likely that means-testing for ability to pay service charges could not be so easily separated from the procedures for establishing need.

Managing front-line discretion

No matter how 'need' was defined it remained the task of front-line staff to manage the conflicting policy aims contained in the barrage of policy and operational guidance accompanying full implementation.

The Audit Commission made it clear that the setting of local priorities for community care was the responsibility of members and officers, not front-line staff (Audit Commission, 1992b, p 26). In keeping with the restructuring of other public services over the late 1980s and 1990s, community care reforms are underpinned by managerial ideals and techniques drawn from the private sector. The emphasis is on the role of the manager rather than the professional in delivering policy objectives.

Managerial control was to be exercised through the greater formalisation and routinisation of assessment practice, aided by the 'invisible monitoring' of new technology (Newman and Clarke, 1994, p 20). Computerised client information systems would be used to 'interrogate' new service requests according to established criteria, and structure their passage through the 'gates' set up at each stage of the assessment and care management system.

However, the primary means of curtailing front-line discretion would be through the devolution of budgets and their management. This was to transform professionals into managers working within tight financial controls (Gray and Jenkins, 1993, p 12).

The role of the social worker

Social workers are generally regarded as the key professional group within social services departments yet they were denied a distinctive role in community care. Official guidance refers to 'practitioners' making no distinction between social workers and other kinds of workers who might be involved in assessment (Cheetham, 1993).

New arrangements for assessment and care management further undermined a traditional social work role in which assessment skills are employed to probe beneath 'presenting problems' and uncover underlying 'need'. The task of the 'practitioner' is not to discover need, but to target resources on people identified as most at risk according to service criteria. The distinction made between 'simple' and 'complex' assessment in guidance challenges long-standing social work approaches to assessment (Cheetham, 1993).

Splitting the assessment function from the 'core' task of purchasing also compromises the long established indivisibility of assessment and service provision in social work. Traditionally, social work assessment has been a process - not just of uncovering needs but of developing an appropriate response to needs as they are discovered. It is a process that is properly conducted in the context of a relationship (Stevenson and

Parsloe, 1993). 'Needs talk' and 'services talk', as Cheetham argues, cannot be rigidly separated, nor is assessment "just a brisk and friendly interview centred on a comprehensive document or a pro forma" (Cheetham, 1993).

The devolution of budgets has perhaps brought the work of the 'practitioner' closer to that of domiciliary care management than social work. The home care organiser has long been accustomed to assessing people's needs for home care hours purchased from a cash-limited budget that they also manage. Certainly, home care organisers interviewed just before full implementation of the NHSCCA felt that they were an occupational group whose time had come. They felt better equipped for the challenges of assessment and care management than social workers whose professional skills and values they regarded as somewhat arcane (Ellis, 1993a).

The aspirations of disabled people

If new arrangements for community care were of concern to professional interest groups, they were also criticised by disability lobby groups for failing to meet the aspirations of disabled people.

In its guidance to practitioners, the SSI suggested that 'need' is "a shorthand for the requirements of individuals to enable them to achieve, maintain or restore an acceptable level of social independence or quality of life, as defined by the particular care agency or authority" (DoH et al, 1991a, p 12). At one level, then, need was linked to what the government identified in policy guidance as the overarching objective of community care reforms, "producing the services and support which will enable people affected by ageing and disability to live as independently as possible" (DoH, 1990, Foreword).

Yet the concept of 'independence' embedded in community care is criticised by the disability lobby for its roots in a medical model of disability. Eligibility criteria are designed less to support personal autonomy than to seek out those most 'dependent' on others for personal 'care', or assistance with daily living tasks. Moreover, people defined according to prioritisation criteria as physically or psychologically 'dependent' may be disqualified from receiving services because they are judged to be receiving a sufficient level of informal support. Measuring need negatively in terms of the extent to which a person could come to significant harm without services means increasing the possibility of enforcing people's dependency on family or friends.

The situation for black and Asian disabled people is even bleaker. As studies have shown, additional barriers are placed in the way of their access to assessment and, therefore, to services. Such barriers are created by forms of service planning and delivery that reflect and recreate racial inequalities and that fail to respond positively to ethnic and cultural diversity (see Ahmad and Atkin, 1996; Butt and Mirza, 1996).

The definition of need offered by the SSI points to its 'social' dimension yet also makes it clear the concept has no meaning outside of service criteria. For the disability movement, social needs are related to educational deprivation, unemployment, poverty and an inaccessible physical environment and transport system. The issues of most significance to disabled people are, therefore, unlikely to be addressed by community care assessments governed by risk-based eligibility criteria.

A survey of prioritisation criteria published in community care plans following full implementation of the NHSCCA indicated that risk to social interaction or community involvement would be routinely accorded the lowest priority by social services departments (Ellis, 1993b). Resourcing levels would reduce the actual meaning of 'social independence' to people's physical safety in their own home. Indeed, the SSI itself set the goal of services no higher than maintaining a 'minimum quality of life' (DoH et al, 1991a, p 53).

Yet disabled people who need services, help or adaptations to live in the community usually have no choice but to attempt to access an assessment. Unless they are comfortably-off, it is the only way for them to gain support.

Rights to assessment

People legally defined as disabled under Section 29 of the 1948 National Assistance Act do retain the right, conferred by previous legislation, to bypass tests of eligibility governing access to differing levels of assessment and obtain a full assessment of need. If a disabled person so requests, local authorities have a duty under the 1986 Disabled Persons (Services,

Consultation and Representation) Act to assess their needs for any of the services listed in Section 2 of the 1970 Chronically Sick and Disabled Persons Act. Section 47(2) of the NHSCCA places a duty on local authorities to advise disabled people of their rights under existing legislation.

A common misconception on the part of local authorities is that these rights apply only to people under the age of 65 with physical or sensory impairments (Parrott, 1990). Yet, given that the definition of a 'disabled person' has no upper age limit and extends to people with learning disabilities and mental health problems, these provisions probably apply to the majority of people served by social services departments. However, a RADAR-sponsored study revealed that many managers and staff were unaware of disabled people's rights under the 1986 Act, believing that they had been superseded by the NHSCCA (Keep et al, 1996).

Nor does the right to access an assessment confer an entitlement to services, particularly since the House of Lords ruling in the Gloucestershire case (R v Gloucestershire County Council and the Secretary of State ex parte Barry, 20 March 1997). Now that it is permissible for local authorities to take account of available resources when matching services to assessed need, they have, in effect, been empowered to tailor assessments to resources available.

Antidiscriminatory policy and practice
The disability lobby has long argued for a shift away from assessing people's needs for services towards upholding their rights to participate in mainstream economic and social life (Morris, 1997). This is linked, in turn, to the long struggle for antidiscriminatory legislation and the 1996 Disability Discrimination Act poses the additional challenge to local authorities of respecting the rights of disabled people to non-discriminatory forms of service.

Since the early 1990s, professional social work training has also included an express commitment to challenge discrimination and oppression through antiracist and antidiscriminatory practice. In the past, social workers have been criticised for basing their practice on a medical or individual model of disability which embodies the assumptions that:

- disabled people's 'problems' are due to their impairments;
- the role of the professional is to help disabled people 'come to terms' with their impairment (Oliver, 1983).

The principles of antidiscriminatory practice require closer adherence to a social model of disability which takes the position that:

- people with impairments are 'disabled' by attitudinal and structural barriers;
- the role of the social worker is to tackle these barriers and work in partnership with disabled people to challenge a discriminatory and 'disabling' community.

Yet the changes that have been made do not provide the social worker with much room for the discretion required to engage in empowering assessment practice. New assessment arrangements reflect a medical model of disability. Eligibility criteria based on measures of risk and dependency encourage assessors to see need in terms of individual impairment rather than socially created discrimination. There is a marked tension here between professional values and agency agendas.

Carers

A further objective of new arrangements for community care was "to ensure service providers make practical support for carers a high priority" (DoH, 1990, para 1.1). Local authorities have a powerful incentive to support carers as they often provide the sort of care that would be very expensive to replace. Good practice therefore dictated that their contribution be formally assessed (DoH et al, 1991a; 1991b).

Where the needs of disabled people and their carers appeared to conflict, the SSI advised a separate assessment of their needs (DoH et al, 1991a; 1991b). The 1995 Carers Recognition and Services Act, introduced while this research was being undertaken, places a duty on local authorities carrying out an assessment under Section 47(1)(a) of the NHSCCA to carry out a separate assessment of a carer's needs if the carer is providing a 'substantial amount of care' on a regular basis and a request is made to the local authority.

Both Acts reinforce the tendency within social services departments to categorise people as either 'users' or 'carers'. This can distort the reality of caring situations. Because reciprocity characterises many caring relationships, it is not always easy to decide who is doing the 'caring' and who is the 'cared for' (Morris, 1993). Categorisation may also obscure the needs of carers who are themselves disabled.

An emphasis on supporting the carer can serve to exaggerate the 'dependency' of the service user, and the imposition of an additional duty to assess on local authorities, without extra funding, may find disabled people competing for assessments with carers. At the same time, previous research would suggest that carers are not so much supported as treated instrumentally by service providers, as a resource at their disposal. Most services provided to 'support' carers are actually a byproduct of interventions directed at the service user (Twigg and Atkin, 1994).

Conclusion

Access to assessment is driven by competing imperatives. The policy rhetoric is of needs-led assessments offering choice and empowerment to disabled people. In reality, however, the concept of 'need' appears to have little meaning outside the prioritisation criteria local authorities construct to stay within budget. The basis of decisions about who accesses an assessment, and of what type and level, therefore seems likely to be a test of eligibility for services.

The majority of people approaching social services departments for help have a statutory right to access a fuller assessment than they will tend to be offered under the new arrangements. Moreover, a central demand of the disability lobby is the right of disabled people to define their own needs, rather than have their access to support made dependent on the decisions of welfare gatekeepers. Ironically, the 1995 Disability Discrimination Act is based on the principle that disabled people have a right to non-discriminatory forms of service, yet access to community care services is itself based on highly restrictive and disablist definitions of 'need', perpetuating people's exclusion from mainstream provision.

The disability movement points to the emptiness of promises of greater 'choice' and 'independence' when services are rationed according to the availability of relatives and friends. The carers' lobby is also suspicious of a rhetorical commitment to supporting carers at a time when the direction of policy has been towards greater reliance on 'family' care. Although carers now also have a statutory right to an assessment, this is dependent on the person they care for satisfying increasingly stringent eligibility tests to access an assessment. The tendency to treat 'users' and 'carers' as mutually exclusive categories increases the likelihood that ever-tighter rationing of resources will place disabled people and their carers in competition with each other to access support.

At the sharp end of the new arrangements are the front-line 'practitioners'. In determining people's access to assessment they must be guided by narrowly focused prioritisation criteria while simultaneously responding to the heightened expectations of disabled people and their carers. Social workers are faced with the additional ethical dilemma of operating according to the principles of antidiscriminatory practice in situations where their discretion has been curtailed and where the very basis of rationing access to assessment runs counter to professional values and aspirations.

The next chapter looks at the structural and operational changes made by the two local authorities studied in order to cope with the contradictions of community care policy and the way differing social work teams managed those tensions at the point of access to assessment and care management systems.

2
Managing access to assessment: the view from the front line

The assumption underlying official guidance was that access to assessment and care management would be governed by a common set of procedures, both within and between local authorities. To ensure 'flexibility', the SSI presented local authority managers with a range of organisational models for implementing new assessment arrangements. Yet, as lead agency, social services departments were also responsible for coordinating the assessment of all community care needs and delivering an equitable service. The expectation, therefore, was that the model - or combination of models - adopted would be governed by a common set of procedures and eligibility criteria, both for determining the type and level of assessment required and for conducting assessments.

The operational manuals of the two local authority social services departments in which this research was conducted were closely based on central government guidance. They suggested that a common set of eligibility criteria and organisational procedures governed access to assessment across the teams included in the study. Yet observation of practice revealed that the basis of eligibility differed between teams, even within the same authority, and that people's access to and experience of assessment varied according to the type of team carrying out the assessment. The diversity of those teams is described in the next section.

The teams

The evidence on which this chapter is based was provided by observation of assessments in six social work teams. In all of these teams most assessment work was undertaken by qualified social workers. In the Younger Person's and Older Person's Teams welfare assistants sometimes undertook assessment work. The Blind Team used rehabilitation officers as well as social workers for assessment. The teams represented a spread of organisational settings, agencies and client groups (excluding mental health services and services for people with learning disabilities). Five of the teams were community-based and the sixth a hospital team. Of the five community-based teams, one was responsible for older people, one for older and younger disabled people, and the other three for people with physical or sensory impairments. One of the latter three teams was a voluntary agency contracted by the local authority to provide assessments on its behalf.

This diversity was further cross-cut by a generic/specialist divide. The Older Person's Team in Authority A was one of four teams covering the geographical 'quarters' of the local authority and the Generic Team in Authority B similarly covered a specific geographic area. The 'specialist' teams, however, the Younger Person's Team in Authority A, the Deaf Team and the Blind Team in Authority B, provided authority-wide cover.

Figure 1: Authority A - flow of cases for assessment and care management

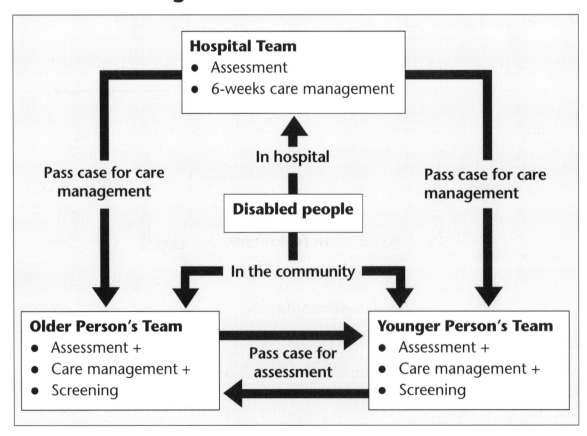

The teams also played different roles in accessing people to the two systems of assessment and care management. In Authority A, the Older Person's Team acted as gatekeeper to other parts of the system, screening referrals on behalf of the 'specialist' teams - although the latter also accepted direct referrals from disabled people and their carers. Figure 1 shows the flow of cases for assessment and care management in local authority A.

The Generic Team in Authority B also screened referrals to the specialist teams although, again, it was possible for disabled people or their carers to approach either of these teams themselves directly.

Figure 2 shows the flow of cases for assessment and care management and referrals in Authority B.

Figure 2: Authority B - flow of cases for assessment and care management

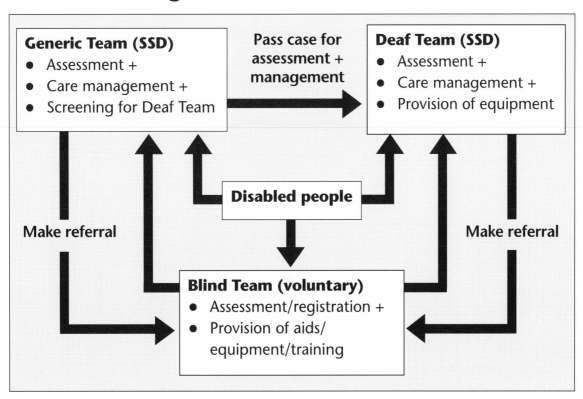

Varying budgetary arrangements further differentiated the assessment responsibilities of the six teams. Following implementation of the NHSCCA, Authority A had rearranged its social work teams into 'Assessment and Care Management Teams'. Both the Older Person's and Younger Person's teams held their own budgets with social workers acting as assessors and care managers, using the team's budget to put together packages of care for the disabled people they assessed.

Social workers on the Hospital Team in Authority A, however, acted as assessors and care managers only for a period of six weeks, after which time cases would be passed to the relevant community-based team for long-term care management. Lacking access to their own budget, they arranged services using budgets belonging to the Younger Person's Team and Older Person's Team, depending on the age of the disabled person being assessed.

Both the Generic Team and the Deaf Team in Authority B had strict budgetary limits to the services they could provide. The Blind Team was a county-wide voluntary organisation to which responsibility for the assessment and registration of blind people had been contracted out. It held a budget for the provision of some services, but had to pass cases for assessment for departmentally funded services to the relevant social services team.

The 'reality gap'

Both managers and social workers expressed the view during observations that eligibility criteria and formal procedures designed to shape their practice failed to take account of the competing tensions they had to resolve in assessment.

First-tier managers felt they had been charged with implementing a top-down structure that did not necessarily closely relate to the reality of front-line practice. Additionally, the period between full implementation of the NHSCCA and the research undertaken for this study had been one of upheaval for managers and front-line workers in both local authorities. This was particularly so in Authority B where, initially, a strict 'purchaser-provider split' had been adopted, with purchasers (social work managers) acting quite separately from service providers, such as home care managers. Just prior to the time the research took place, however, this split had been dissolved, and the link between purchasers and providers of services restored.

Changes in organisational structure, policies, procedures and practices had entailed significant changes in the location, content and, sometimes, title of jobs for both managers and front-line staff in the two authorities. Yet front-line staff complained that they had received very little training in their new roles and responsibilities.

Observation of practice suggests that similar strategies to managing the contradictory tasks of assessment had been adopted in the Older Person's/Generic, Specialist and Hospital Teams respectively. The rest of

Table 1: The formal criteria for assessment in the Generic and Older Person's Team

	The Generic Team	The Older Person's Team
Who is eligible for an assessment?	People at immediate or imminent risk of harm, who have insufficient informal care - people at a 'lower' risk will only be assessed once everyone at the 'higher' level of risk has received services	People who are 'vulnerable', or are asking for an assessment under the 1986 Disabled Person's Act
When is this decided?	During the 'initial' assessment undertaken by the duty social worker	During 'screening' undertaken by a duty social worker or welfare assistant (the assessment does not officially begin until after this stage)
Are there different levels of assessment?	Yes, according to how many levels of the computerised record system need to be filled in. After the 'initial' assessment, a 'further' assessment is carried out if the person ends up receiving services, and a 'full' assessment if some liaison with other agencies is necessary, or a complicated 'package' of services is needed	Yes, there are three levels of assessment (simple, direct and comprehensive) according to their level of risk and whether they have 'complex' needs

the chapter examines the distinct approaches to negotiating access to assessment found within these three types of team and the implications this had for choice and participation by disabled people.

The Older Person's/Generic Teams
The basis of eligibility

The key determinants of access to an assessment by these teams were the formal eligibility criteria set out in Table 1. The basis of eligibility was 'risk' and access was determined, in effect, by a person's predicted need for a service provided or funded by the local authority concerned.

Eligibility criteria were also used to determine the urgency of referrals. People considered to be most at risk received an assessment within 24 hours to a week whereas those judged to be at a lower risk had to wait for anything up to several months for an assessment.

Access to assessment was further dependent on the funding for services being available. Both teams performed assessments within the framework of devolved budgets and eligibility criteria in the Generic Team were explicitly linked to the budget held by the team (see Table 1). As Example 1 demonstrates, this could exclude some disabled people from accessing an assessment.

Example 1

During the period of this study, local authority B experienced a staffing crisis that meant the Generic Team would lose a member of staff to another team without a replacement. When this issue was raised at a team meeting, concern was expressed that this would add to the waiting time for assessments for those people considered to be at a lower risk. One worker was worried that this would create an unmanageable waiting list for assessments. Her manager replied that this would not be the case - people at a lower risk would simply not receive an assessment at all. He justified this by saying there was no point making people wait for assessments if there was unlikely to be any money to offer them a service.

The majority of people approaching these teams for assistance would be likely to fall within the legal definition of 'disabled'. Yet the Generic Team made no mention of a right to an assessment in its formal procedures or official eligibility criteria. Practitioners on both teams seemed unaware of disabled people's legal rights to assessment and services.

Access to assessment

Screening

Enquiries in both authorities were screened by reception staff. People had to satisfy this preliminary test of eligibility if they were to proceed through to the first stage of assessment - the 'initial' assessment. People opening with an enquiry about housing, benefits, or other concerns dealt with by another agency would usually be advised to contact that organisation direct. Often people who were referred on in this way turned out to have relevant enquiries and would then be advised to get back in contact with the team.

'Initial' assessment

People successfully negotiating the receptionists' screening still had to get through the 'initial' assessment. This was usually carried out over the 'phone by a duty social worker. As Table 1 indicates, it was at this stage that the process of identifying 'need' officially began. However, observation of practice suggests that the key function of the 'initial' assessment was to test people's eligibility for a further assessment and/or services rather than explore their perceptions of their needs.

During an 'initial assessment', duty social workers would usually centre their questions on the health and, particularly, the mobility of the enquirer to try and establish whether they were at risk. Follow-up telephone calls would be made to other professionals (such as GPs, occupational therapists and community nurses) and/or informal carers to supplement the information received from, or more likely about, the person concerned. Such probing tended to be negatively directed towards uncovering evidence that might disqualify the person from receiving a service.

Because eligibility was determined on the basis of available services, people would be asked which service they required during the 'initial' assessment. Even if they didn't know, duty social workers would still relate their questions directly to services provided or funded by the local authority to avoid the danger of identifying needs that couldn't be met within the budget.

Accessing a further assessment

Duty social workers had the option of carrying out a 'screening visit' if a decision about the priority to be accorded to a referral could not be made on the evidence available. However, this alternative was used sparingly as it was generally considered possible to gather enough information during the 'initial' assessment to judge how to proceed. It was therefore possible for duty social workers to carry out an assessment without ever meeting the disabled person face to face or, indeed, without the person concerned being aware that an assessment had taken place.

When determining the type and level of any additional assessment resources to be applied, duty social workers would refer to further assessments by their service name - for example, a 'Home Care Assessment', or a 'Day Care Assessment'. Enquirers unable to frame their request appropriately made little progress.

Example 2

A hospital nurse phoned the team to ask for an assessment for one of her patients. The duty social worker asked the nurse what service the patient needed. The nurse said she wasn't sure; she thought it was the social worker's job to do the needs assessment and establish what the patient needed. The social worker asked impatiently what the nurse meant by a needs assessment - did she mean a Home Care Assessment, or Day Care Assessment? The nurse thought the patient might need home care, but wanted the social worker to visit the patient to assess whether that was what he needed. The social worker decided that the patient needed a 'Home Care Assessment', and referred him to the home care manager.

Duty social workers would frequently refer people on for a 'home care assessment' on the basis of an 'initial' assessment carried out over the telephone. This was also used as a means of screening people for other services thereby rationing access to a 'full' assessment - or face-to-face visit by a social worker.

Limiting access

The 'initial' assessment was the lynch-pin of these teams' assessment and care management systems, fulfilling the objective of 'targeting' assessments and services on the most needy - or those judged to be at immediate, or potential, risk of harm without the provision of services - and preventing the majority of people from proceeding any further. This aim was symbolically underlined by the physical location of the two teams. Both were housed in inaccessible buildings and worked behind number-locked doors. Few disabled people ever visited and there were no disabled members of staff. Indeed, a disabled student social worker had had to end her placement on one of the teams because of the inaccessibility of the building.

The social work role

While social workers believed new arrangements actively encouraged a service-led approach to assessment, they were keen to emphasise that their core professional skills around assessment had survived intact. They strongly objected to the term 'rationing' being applied to the initial stages of assessment, insisting that their professional involvement ensured an assessment of need took place even if all that happened was that an enquirer was referred onto another agency.

Some social workers expressed reservations about the diversion of referrals directly to home care, believing everyone could benefit from a fuller, expert assessment. For example, there would be occasional references to the 'family conflicts' suspected to lie beneath the surface of referral information. However, these concerns were unlikely to be followed up unless they represented an obvious risk.

Further, the majority of social workers were comfortable with the division of labour around assessment, justifying it in terms of saving their costly expertise for more 'complex' work. Observation of practice, however, suggests that assessment was rarely used as a tool of professional practice - to advocate, promote self-determination, build relationships, explore need and develop responses appropriate to the particular circumstances of individuals and households.

Formalisation of assessment

Operational procedures shaping front-line practice in these two teams acted as a disincentive for social workers to use their specialist expertise in assessment. The computerised information system used by the Generic Team, for example, 'rewarded' social workers for minimalist responses. Any telephone conversation, regardless of whether any further action was taken, could be logged as an 'initial' assessment. These would be added to the number of completed assessments recorded by the team without the social worker having to meet the person concerned or carry out a 'full' assessment.

To qualify as a 'full' assessment, the disabled person had to end up receiving a local authority-funded service. Given that no significant space was provided in the system to record any other sort of work, there was an inbuilt disincentive for social workers to spend time on anyone who didn't appear to need, or be eligible for, the limited list of services provided or funded by the local authority. Ultimately, workers were being encouraged to carry out service-led assessments.

Social workers expressed some resentment at computerised systems, seeing time spent on inputting client details as time away from their core business of needs assessment. They also believed collaborative working was undermined by the requirement for one member of staff to 'own' each case logged on the system.

There was some nostalgia for the old paperwork systems which social workers perceived as connecting more closely to people's needs. What appeared to frustrate them was the way in which computerised systems constructed assessment as a linear sequence of interrelated decisions about eligibility. For social workers, assessment was a process of human interaction and the order in which information emerged could not therefore be mechanistically predetermined.

Denying participation and choice

Disabled people tended to play the least important part in identifying their needs. As indicated, a fairly detailed assessment could be carried out over the telephone without the disabled person ever being involved. In addition to using outside professionals, social workers were particularly reliant on carers for information about an individual's needs. This was often gathered over the telephone without the knowledge of the disabled person concerned.

So far from advocating on behalf of disabled people, duty social workers would actively use eligibility criteria to dissuade people from taking their enquiry further. It would be made clear to people considered to have a lower level of need that they would only access an assessment if everyone with a higher level of need had received one. People assessed as not at risk were discouraged from wasting scarce resources.

Practitioners also used service charging policies as an informal tool of rationing. All the teams in this study had introduced or increased service charges following full implementation of the NHSCCA. Practitioners on these two teams made a point of explaining the service charges during the initial contact. The necessity for a 'financial assessment' indirectly dissuaded people unwilling to reveal personal information about income and savings from proceeding further.

If disabled people or carers specifically asked for a service that was not available from the local authority, practitioners would sometimes try to persuade them to buy it privately. This was particularly likely to happen if the enquirers appeared to be well off, or were asking about housework or 'pop-in' services (which check on people, rather than undertake any personal care).

Reinforcing dependency

Even when a local authority funded service was available, duty social workers might still attempt to persuade people they could manage for themselves or buy in their own care.

Example 3

A duty social worker received a telephone call from Mrs A, a middle-aged woman who wanted someone to collect her pension because of her agoraphobia. Her daughter lived with her and was in full-time education. The worker asked whether her daughter could collect her pension. It turned out her daughter was never around during the day when the Post Office was open. The worker asked, rather sceptically, how many hours a week of education the daughter received. Was it not possible for her daughter to collect her pension when she wasn't in college? Mrs A reiterated that it wasn't. In that case, the worker advised Mrs A it would be better for her to pay an agency privately as the local authority home care service was overstretched. After she had hung up the phone, the social worker told the researcher providing a local authority service would "reinforce Mrs A's dependency."

This example illustrates the particular meaning that 'dependency' can take on in teams adopting a predominantly 'rationing' stance towards assessment. As a potential drain on resources, Mrs A was assessed as requesting a service she didn't really need. Because 'need' is seen in terms of resource use, a judgement of moral worthiness is implied. This in turn serves to reinforce an individualistic concept of 'independence', rooted in norms of self-sufficiency and able-bodiedness, according to which impairment is routinely confirmed as the source of disability.

The role of carers

For a disabled person to be assessed as 'needy' carried negative financial and moral connotations. Visibly stressed but coping carers, however, could be judged both 'needy' and 'worthy' of assistance. In one case the researcher observed a 'full' assessment offered to a woman who was caring for her elderly mother at the same time as fostering a young girl and looking after her own children. Even though the carer's mother was not at risk (the criterion for receiving a 'full' assessment) the social worker felt the carer needed some support.

Carers tended to be accorded a dominant role in assessments carried out by these two teams, particularly if the disabled person made it through to a 'full' assessment. At this stage too, information could be gathered without the knowledge of the disabled person, by social workers only talking to carers. The only time carers risked exclusion from an assessment was where they were themselves disabled. The assumption seemed to be that only an able-bodied member of the family could be a carer.

Of course this willingness to support carers can be related to the overall 'rationing' stance of these teams. Carers were a valued resource who required support to prevent a need for higher levels of formal support developing. This could reinforce the prioritisation of their needs during assessment encounters.

Example 4

Mr W was an older man who hated going into respite residential care. He hated the food and having to receive help with personal care from strangers. He also objected to paying for respite care when he had such a miserable time. However, his wife, Mrs W, found caring for him very hard work. She felt he was too demanding and had unrealistic expectations of respite care. She badly needed the break that respite care gave her. Mr W disagreed with his wife's view that caring for him was hard work. The social worker assessing Mr W persuaded him to carry on using respite to give his wife a break. The worker felt it was important to support Mrs W in this way to prevent 'carer breakdown'.

Operational guidance stipulated that an assessment could not take place without the disabled person's consent but, as the next example shows, this would not necessarily ensure a key role for the disabled person.

Example 5

Mr B was an older man who was in hospital following a collapse due to over-medication. He was still feeling very 'woozy' and confused when his assessment took place. His wife asked the social worker if Mr B could have a bath when he went to day care. The social worker told her that there was a waiting list for that service (known as a 'tea 'n' tub'). Mr B pointed out that there was a bath at home - why couldn't he use that? Mrs B said she couldn't bath Mr B at home without a walk-in bath. An auxiliary nurse present at the assessment added that the nurse couldn't get Mr B into a normal bath either. The social worker, auxiliary nurse and Mrs B all agreed that Mr B would have to go on the waiting list for the 'tea 'n' tub' session. Mr B protested that this was a waste with a 'perfectly good bath tub at home'. His protests were put down to his confusion and ignored.

Because Mr B was ignored, the social worker failed to consider alternatives (such as a lift into the bath) that would enable him to have his bath at home. His carer's view that he was better off having a bath at day care was given greater weight, a view that also, of course, articulated with the overall 'rationing' stance of the teams reviewed here.

Unless disabled people were very assertive at putting forward their point of view, social workers would often make little effort to include them, other than to ask if they agreed with their carer. As both examples in this section indicate, older disabled people were particularly vulnerable in this respect.

The specialist teams
Basis of eligibility

According to the operational manuals used by the specialist teams, access to an assessment was also governed by eligibility criteria based on risk. However, two further criteria were frequently more significant in securing access:

- the age/impairment criteria of the team concerned;
- the legal status of the applicant as a 'disabled person'.

In the case of the Younger Person's Team, the client group was defined in terms of age whereas the client groups of the Blind Team and the Deaf Team were identified in terms of primary impairment. To access an assessment by the latter teams, therefore, applicants had to have the 'right' impairment. One member of the Blind Team faced with a list of questions from a disabled person she was assessing maintained "I can only help you if it's to do with your sight".

As Table 2 shows, eligibility criteria for the specialist teams formally acknowledged the teams' legal obligations to assess members of their respective constituencies. The Younger Person's Team recognised the rights of people with a physical impairment who met the age criterion to access an assessment under the 1986 Disabled Persons Act. The Blind Team was responsible for the formal registration of people as blind or partially sighted and used the same process for assessment as for registration.

Because people fitting the age and impairment related criteria of the teams were seen to be *entitled* to an assessment, there was far less emphasis in these teams on disabled people satisfying risk-related eligibility criteria. The exception was older people. As on the teams discussed earlier, their access to a particular type and level of assessment appeared far more likely to be judged in terms of their predicted requirement for services, regardless of their primary impairment or legal status as 'disabled'.

Table 2: The formal criteria for assessment in the specialist teams

	The Deaf Team	The Blind Team	The Younger Person's Team
Who is eligible for an assessment?	Deaf adults and children	People who are blind or partially sighted	People who are 'vulnerable', or are asking for an assessment under the 1986 Disabled Person's Act
When is this decided?	During the 'initial' assessment undertaken by the duty social worker	By the receptionist on the initial enquiry	During 'screening' undertaken by a duty social worker or welfare assistant (the assessment does not officially begin until after this stage)
Are there different levels of assessment?	Yes, according to how many levels of the computerised record system need to be filled in. After the 'initial' assessment, a 'further' assessment is carried out if the person ends up receiving services, and a 'full' assessment if some liaison with other agencies is necessary, or a complicated 'package' of services is needed	No	Yes, there are three levels of assessment (simple, direct and comprehensive) according to their level of risk and whether they have 'complex' needs

The specialist teams were also less restricted by departmental eligibility criteria because they had access to resources outside the limited menu of services supplied or funded by the local authority. The Blind Team, for example, held a large stock of equipment or services (such as training to use long canes, or learn Braille) to which the team had access. Because of their charitable status, the team could offer this equipment and training free of charge to most people. Indeed, people assessed by this team could sometimes be overwhelmed by what was on offer - an unlikely occurrence elsewhere.

Access to assessment
Open access

The basis of eligibility created a pressure to offer an assessment to everyone referred to a specialist team; and these teams received a higher level of self-referrals than the other two types included in the study. With the exception of older people, therefore, risk-based eligibility criteria were used less to exclude people from accessing a further assessment than to determine the speed with which it was carried out.

Lack of staff meant it was necessary to operate waiting lists. The Younger Person's Team and the Deaf Team operated a priority system - urgent referrals were dealt with as soon as possible, less urgent ones could wait months. The waiting time for an assessment by the Blind Team was largely dictated by staff members' workload, although people could jump the queue if they were considered to need an assessment urgently. This usually meant they were deemed to be at risk - of burning themselves while cooking, for example.

Making assessment accessible

In the specialist teams, access to assessment was as much about ensuring people had the means actively to participate in their assessment as it was about gatekeeping departmental resources. Information was key. The Deaf Team had created its own sign-language video about the assessment process. The Blind Team sent out leaflets explaining the registration process prior to their visit and attempted to demystify the process during the assessment visit.

It was also standard practice in all the specialist teams to make it clear that, if the disabled person had any further questions, staff could be contacted after the assessment visit. Members of the Blind Team would leave a 'summary of assessment' form with details of how to contact them when they left. This was distinct from a care plan, which would only be provided if a disabled person was actually receiving local authority-funded services.

Making assessment accessible was a time-consuming business. It was not easy to accomplish it in one visit, particularly if the client was new. Consequently, many assessments carried out by the specialist teams happened over more than one visit. The Deaf Team had the added task of making sure the person being assessed was not excluded on linguistic grounds. Deaf workers would often spend most of their first visit establishing communication, before they went on to identify needs.

The emphasis on accessibility rather than eligibility was also reflected in the physical location of the specialist teams. By contrast with the Older Person's and Generic Teams, all the specialist teams worked in buildings with fairly open access.

The social work role
Conflicting tasks of assessment

As discussed in the previous chapter, assessment presents social workers with a number of conflicting tasks. In particular, they have to manage the tension between testing people's eligibility for services and taking account of expressed needs and preferences. Whereas the assessment practice of the Older Person's and Generic Teams was dominated by the former, social workers on the specialist teams were more explicitly committed to promoting participation and the exercise of choice by their respective client groups.

Principles underlying assessment practice

This commitment can be related, in part, to the value base of social work. An emphasis on ensuring participation articulates with a professional objective of promoting self-determination.

Social workers also attached importance to the *qualitative* aspects of assessment, such as building up a relationship of trust with clients. In line with received wisdom within the profession, assessment was perceived as a process taking place over time rather than a discrete event. A professional concern for the *quality* of assessments had not been squeezed out by an emphasis on the *quantity* of assessment outputs to the extent observed on the teams discussed earlier where contacts resulting in no further action literally counted. This concern was directly linked to the goal of promoting participation. Social workers stressed the importance of allowing disabled people the time to discuss their concerns and to dictate the pace and scope of the assessment.

Specialist social workers also had an awareness of and commitment to a social model of disability. In this they were supported by their managers. Unlike the other teams included in the study, all the specialist teams employed disabled people in a range of professional, vocational and support posts. Non-disabled colleagues were forced to re-evaluate their assessment practice in the light of challenges to their attitudes and assumptions from disabled colleagues.

Additionally, several members of specialist teams were involved in leading workshops with local schools and service providers as a way of tackling discriminatory and 'disablist' attitudes locally. The Deaf Team was particularly keen to address the linguistic discrimination experienced by Deaf people.

A commitment to a social model of disability meant that social workers interpreted their role quite widely. They tried to use the assessment to tackle some of the barriers faced by disabled people in society. Some of these barriers were the attitudes and values that disabled people and their families held about disability.

Example 6

Mrs A was an older woman. She was afraid to go out alone because a loss of sight meant that she could not see the kerb and was scared she would fall. The practitioner suggested that Mrs A could be trained to use a 'long cane' - a collapsible white stick that can be used to feel the edge of kerbs and steps. Mrs A said she didn't want a white stick - she didn't want people staring at her, and she didn't want to be "condemned as blind". The practitioner explained that the white stick was an aid, designed to increase Mrs A's independence. If people have a problem with it they need to address their own attitudes. Mrs A said she had never thought of it like that before.

The perspective on disability adopted by the specialist social workers was at variance with the more traditional, medical model used by other professionals inside and outside the department. Consequently, unlike social workers on the Older Person's and Generic Teams who used the views of other professionals on disabled people's needs strategically to confirm or challenge eligibility, the specialist teams treated such sources of information with caution.

Advocacy

Social workers on the specialist teams would also position themselves as advocates, offering disabled people ideas on how to get services from other agencies, such as speeding up housing enquiries by getting a doctor's letter, or applying for disability-related benefits by concentrating on their worst day. Disabled people often appreciated this - they saw the practitioners as being on their side and helping them negotiate some tricky encounters with the various arms of the welfare state. The importance of this to disabled people and carers has been noted in other studies (Twigg and Atkin, 1994).

Overcoming service limitations

Social workers in the Younger Person's Team and the Deaf Team were keenly aware of the limitations of local authority-provided or -funded services. People had to meet certain criteria in order to access these services (for example, needing help with personal care in order to get a home help), and there was little the teams could do to alter this. However, as the following example shows, social workers would try within the overall constraints of available services to explore creative alternatives with the disabled person.

Example 7

Mr H was an older Chinese man who found it extremely difficult to breathe. Mrs H was also in poor health and was finding it very difficult to care for her husband when his chest infections got worse. Neither of them spoke any English. They thought their main difficulty was linguistic - how could they contact help when they needed it? The social worker said she understood that contacting a home help would be a problem. She suggested that Mr H employ a Cantonese speaking personal care assistant, using money set up for them in a trust fund by the social services department. Mr H was unsure about this - his need was so variable, and employing someone would take time. The social worker promised to try and sort it out for him. In the meantime, she arranged a signal with the home care manager that Mr and Mrs H could use to start an emergency home care service, when they needed it.

Although social workers on the specialist teams were restricted by limited budgets, or access to limited services, in contrast to workers on the Older Person's and Generic Teams, they tended to be very open about acknowledging service limitations. This in turn meant that unmet need would be recognised. Although the Younger Person's Team and the Older Person's Team shared the same eligibility criteria, the following example helps illustrate the differing approach to unmet need adopted by the two teams.

Example 8

Mrs L was a young woman who lived with a husband (who worked full time) and her three children. She had multiple sclerosis and when she was very tired found caring for her children extremely difficult. She contacted the social worker to ask for extra help with childcare. However, because the extra help was not required for her own care, there was nothing the social worker could offer. Because Mrs L's children were not at risk, there was nothing the Children and Families Team could offer her. The social worker promised to record this as unmet need.

In this situation the social worker is confronted with a request for a service she cannot meet given departmental eligibility criteria. Rather than responding to the request by pointing to a scarcity of resources, or by suggesting Mrs L purchases care privately, the social worker formally acknowledges the validity of the request by recording it as unmet need.

The more imaginative approach of the specialist teams can also be linked to the extent to which they were much more clearly a part of a wider network of provision. The Younger Person's Team would put people in touch with local self-operated care schemes or enable people to buy in and manage their own care with trust funds financed through the Independent Living Fund. The Deaf Team had links to Deaf consumer councils and county-wide deaf clubs that opened up access to the Deaf community. The Blind Team had access to a large voluntary network run by the charity, which could offer a range of flexible services.

The role of carers

The commitment to ensuring disabled people's voices were heard in assessment influenced social workers' interaction with carers. The Deaf Team, for example, often found themselves in conflict with family members who would not use sign language to communicate.

Specialist social workers were generally careful not to let carers speak for disabled people. However, when confronted with older disabled people considered to be at risk, workers could adopt a different tack and abandon their explicit defence of disabled people's wishes. Carers would be used by social workers to identify the disabled person's needs, even if this went against the disabled person's wishes.

Example 9

Mr B, an older man, asked if he could have an extra rail put in his bathroom. The social worker examined the bathroom and said he was not happy about Mr B's safety in there because of Mr B's poor eyesight and mobility problems. Mr B thought his safety could be improved by an extra rail but didn't want any more help. He particularly did not want a home care assistant because of the cost, as he had money worries. The social worker said he was concerned that Mr B was at risk, and he wanted to involve his two sons in the assessment. Mr B was unwilling to give the social worker his sons' telephone numbers - he didn't want them bothered at work and he didn't want them to worry about him. The social worker refused to continue with the assessment until Mr B agreed to let him contact his sons.

The social worker justified his actions to the researcher by saying that his professional training put him in a better position to judge Mr B's risk than Mr B himself.

The Hospital Team
The basis of eligibility

According to the operational manual, the same set of procedures governed access to an assessment by the Hospital Team as any other team in Authority A (see Table 3). However, the Hospital Team was under considerable and continuous pressure from hospital management to avoid 'bed-blocking', or tying up a hospital bed by delaying a patient's discharge. Frequently, therefore, it was how close the person was to being discharged rather than risk-based eligibility criteria that determined whether and how quickly he or she received a social work assessment.

Table 3: The formal criteria for assessment in the Hospital Team	
	The Hospital Team
Who is eligible for an assessment?	People who are 'vulnerable', or are asking for an assessment under the 1986 Disabled Person's Act
When is this decided?	During 'screening' undertaken by a duty social worker or welfare assistant (the assessment does not officially begin until after this stage)
Are there different levels of assessment?	Yes, there are three levels of assessment (simple, direct and comprehensive) according to their level of risk and whether they have 'complex' needs

Because a speedy discharge often depended on the availability of social care, eligibility for an assessment by the Hospital Team was further determined by a prediction about the requirement for services. Referrals for a comprehensive assessment made on behalf of people who were mobile and 'self-caring' were usually regarded as inappropriate because there was no obvious need for the services offered by the local authority.

As was the case on the Older Person's Team, the reference in departmental eligibility criteria to disabled people's statutory entitlement to access an assessment was generally ignored. Because eligibility was tied to a requirement for a narrow set of services people who were not obviously disabled (or had impairments that didn't affect their mobility or ability to carry out their own personal care) were denied an assessment of their needs.

Access to assessment
Accessing the team
Most requests for assessments came to the social work team from hospital nurses via a formal referral system. Disabled people or their carers who wanted an assessment therefore had to rely on nurses to make a referral for them. People who approached the team direct were advised to go through the proper referral system lest the paperwork get lost.

The scope for 'self-referral' by relatives visiting the office was further limited by the physical location of the Hospital Team. The team was housed in a temporary office protected by a number lock. There was no reception or waiting area. Team members expressed concern that visitors might overhear something that breached patient confidentiality, let alone threatened their own privacy and safety.

Screening
When a request for an assessment was received, social workers would phone the ward to 'screen' the request. It was at this stage that decisions were made about the relative priority of requests and the type and level of assessment required. As in the Generic and Older Person's Teams, decisions about the latter were based on predicted service use. Only people deemed to have very complex needs or, more usually, people requiring nursing or residential care, gained access to a 'full' or 'comprehensive' assessment. The majority of assessments carried out by the Hospital Team were 'low-level' assessments leading to the provision of a limited package of specific forms of service on discharge.

The assessment of need did not officially begin until *after* the 'screening' stage (see Table 3). In practice, though, social workers were under pressure to speed up the process of discharge from the moment a request from the ward was received. Social workers would question nursing staff about a patient's health, prognosis and likely discharge date both over the telephone and on the ward just prior to the assessment visit. Because this information was used to decide whether the person was 'vulnerable', and hence eligible for services, part of the assessment had been accomplished before the social worker ever met the person concerned.

Social workers tended to defer to nurses' professional judgement, particularly in respect of mobility and health problems. Given that disabled people were unlikely to be consulted during the 'screening' stage, they could find key decisions had been made before they ever saw the social worker.

The social work role

A Hospital Team manager asserted that "everyone gets as comprehensive an assessment as their needs dictate and we assess everyone." Social workers similarly believed that each visit to a patient on the ward constituted an assessment of need rather than a test of eligibility. They felt they were performing an important screening function and stressed the importance of a needs-led social work assessment as a preliminary to the service-led assessments of providers such as home care supervisors.

Yet hospital social workers were essentially performing the 'initial assessment' role of duty social workers on the Generic and Older Person's Teams without the same ready facility to refer 'simple' requests onto the home care team. At the same time, hospital social workers were under the additional and considerable pressure of ensuring services were in place quickly enough to secure a speedy discharge. In practice, therefore, social workers appeared to assess 'need' primarily in terms of available services, particularly home care.

Service-led assessments

The chief purpose of the ward visit seemed to be to assess whether people required home care and to check that they were receiving all their benefits. Accordingly, questions were usually confined to patients' mobility and ability to undertake 'personal care' (washing, dressing and showering).

Social workers would sometimes ask a home care manager to join them at the assessment meeting to ensure the service was available. Once people were discharged from hospital they found that home care managers were reassessing them and changing their agreed service. Social workers were concerned about this practice, ironically because they felt that assessments carried out by home care supervisors were bound to be 'service-led' rather than 'needs-led'.

Yet lack of time and budgetary freedom meant that social workers tended to rely on their knowledge of available services to make decisions about disabled people's needs. Because the typical social work assessment was in effect 'service-led', workers disliked being asked for unavailable services. The most often requested unavailable service was housework. When this service was requested, social workers had been instructed by senior managers to give people a list of private agencies and tell them to sort it out themselves.

Recording unmet need was similarly resisted because it involved acknowledging needs that could not be met. It was also just another piece of paperwork when time was a resource in short supply. Social workers' most common response to unmet need identified in assessment was to try to persuade people they did not require the support requested, often appealing to their professional judgement as the basis for legitimating the refusal.

Example 10

Mrs K was a younger Asian woman having chemotherapy who wanted a period of convalescence before returning home. She was very worried about being a burden on her husband and wanted to regain some of her strength. However, the social worker had been unable to find any convalescent placements suitable for someone as young as Mrs K except one that cost much more than the local authority would pay. The social worker then tried to persuade Mrs K that she was just feeling depressed by the hospital, and that she would feel better once she got home and was surrounded by her family. Mrs K explained that after her chemotherapy being surrounded by her family was the worst possible environment - her mother-in-law would take over and make her feel very dependent. She badly wanted to be stronger before she went home to be able to cope. The worker persuaded Mrs K to go home and get some counselling for her depression.

Low participation

Social workers insisted on meeting the disabled person face to face to carry out the assessment in every possible case; and, according to their procedures manual, they were obliged to take disabled people's preferences into account during the assessment. Social workers would refuse to carry out assessment on anyone who could not participate fully. If the disabled person needed an interpreter, the assessment would be delayed until one was available even where this might contribute towards 'bed-blocking'.

In practice, though, the impetus to undertake assessments as quickly as possible was stronger than the impetus to allow disabled people the space to participate in their assessment and exercise choice. Social workers would often have to carry out an assessment and set up a full package of services to enable a patient to be discharged within five or six hours. Consequently, the ward visit was typically very brief with social workers visiting four to five people within a couple of hours and spending no more than a few minutes with each person.

The ephemeral nature of the assessment visit meant that disabled people often had difficulty distinguishing the social worker from the many health professionals they saw (see Baldock and Ungerson, 1994). Further, only the few people accessing a full assessment were assigned to one worker. People receiving 'low-level' assessments could see three or four different social workers. Staff did not bother to introduce themselves by name (just as a 'duty social worker') as they knew they would be unlikely to be speaking to the person again.

Social workers also tended to rely on what health professionals told them about a patient's medical condition to reach a decision about the service required, rather than on the perceptions of disabled people. As on the Generic and Older Person's Teams, social workers on the Hospital Team were making judgements about risk in functional terms - and this is, after all, the first language of health professionals.

Example 11

Mrs K was a younger Asian woman, who was having problems using her left arm because she had a tumour that was pressing on the nerves. She wanted help to get washed and dressed, particularly washing her hair. Her husband worked away from home and her daughters provided unreliable help. The social worker checked with the ward nurse, who felt that Mrs K's tumour wasn't that big and she was "overly concerned about some numbness." The social worker then told Mrs K she would have to check the availability of services before she could promise anything - Mrs K had been discharged by the time this had been done.

The social worker based her judgement of how urgently Mrs K needed services on the expert view of the nurse rather than on how Mrs K perceived her own needs.

Advocacy

But social workers would invoke the principles of advocacy if the disabled person was perceived as a social services department client whose interests required defending against the hospital management. Despite the pressures to discharge patients as quickly as possible, social workers made an explicit attempt to place themselves on the side of disabled people. In this they were supported by their procedures manual. As a team manager put it, their job was to "support the citizens of A who happen to be in hospital."

Social workers would also advocate for disabled people in conflict with healthcare professionals about how much care was required or about the risk of going home early. Social workers would try to protect people under pressure from nurses or occupational therapists to accept services they were unhappy about. Health professionals were particularly keen for people to have a lot of home care if this seemed likely to prevent the person having to return to hospital. The hospital social workers, however, felt it was up to disabled people themselves to decide how much risk was acceptable. Of course, given their gatekeeping role, this stout defence of patients' rights can also be related to budgetary contingencies.

The role of carers

Social workers' advocacy sometimes extended to supporting disabled people who appeared to be in conflict with family members, particularly carers or potential carers. Relatives could find themselves obliged to provide care because the disabled person refused to accept services; and social workers implicitly encouraged family members to take on the role of carer rather than supported them to refuse it.

Family members were an important component of 'packages of care' designed to ensure safe and speedy discharge. Social workers would sometimes telephone family members at the 'screening' stage, particularly if they had requested the assessment. If it seemed appropriate (for example, if it seemed likely that family members would be providing a lot of care) they would arrange a face to face assessment meeting with the family and the disabled person.

The necessary speed of assessment visits meant carers could come to dominate the proceedings. Disabled people were also frequently too ill, or too worried about their medical prognosis to provide workers with all the information they needed. They often just wanted to get home but had difficulty thinking in abstract terms about what help they might need at home while in the protected environment of the hospital. Social workers would therefore often delay assessments until a carer could be present. They would also speak to carers separately if it reduced the intrusion experienced by disabled people who were very ill. While social workers were explicitly advocating for disabled people, they implicitly allowed carers - as well as other professionals - a greater say in the assessment.

This could place carers in a difficult position. They could be asked to identify a disabled person's needs, which put them in a strong position in the assessment process. However, they could also find themselves unwillingly drawn into the assessment process. If a disabled person refused services, or refused to pay for services, the carer could find themselves in the position of having to provide care.

Example 12

Mrs S was a 93-year-old Irish woman who had been admitted to hospital with pneumonia. Her doctor considered her prognosis was poor. The social worker had asked her two step-daughters to be present for the assessment. The social worker felt that Mrs S should consider going into residential care. Mrs S refused - she said she didn't want to sit around with a "load of old people". The social worker then asked Mrs S to consider having some home care. Mrs S refused - she had had home care before, and "a young girl just came round to watch my television". She refused to pay someone to do that. The social worker then asked the step-daughters if they could care for Mrs S. They were upset at this - they already did much of Mrs S's washing, cleaning and cooking and did not feel that they could cope with anymore. However they felt they had little choice as Mrs S was refusing any outside help.

Conclusion

Contrary to the centralising thrust of policy and operational guidance, the teams observed in this study managed access to assessment in different ways. Neither a common set of formal criteria nor shared professional values ensured a common approach to assessment across the six teams. Eligibility was determined in different ways on the three types of team identified and this helped determine whether disabled people accessed assessment and, if so, what type of assessment they received.

Gaining access to assessment

On the Older Person's and Generic Teams, eligibility was determined primarily in terms of risk-based service criteria, linked in turn to cash-limited budgets. These two teams had primary responsibility for the largest group of potential service users, older people. They were positioned at key points of entry to authority-wide systems of assessment and care management, acting as a filter for people seeking access to other teams. A perceived vulnerability to the ever-present danger of opening the floodgates of pent-up demand meant that procedures for gaining access to assessment were designed to have a deterrent effect.

The specialist teams were less vulnerable to the risk of unpredictable demand. Additionally, these teams were part of a network of local resources on which they could draw to develop 'packages' of services. Consequently, eligibility was not so closely bound to predicted requirement for services provided or funded by the local authorities concerned.

The specialist teams could give fuller expression to people's legal entitlement to access assessment, reflected in the far higher rates of self-referral for assessment on these teams than others included in the study. This was reinforced by the clearer identity of younger people with impairments as 'disabled'. People applying for assistance from the Older Person's and Generic Teams had a primary identity of 'elderly' rather than 'disabled' - two somewhat mutually exclusive identities in social services departments.

Eligibility for an assessment by the Hospital Team was related not to a person's legal status as 'disabled' but to a prediction about whether services provided or funded by the local authority were required. However, eligibility was further shaped by the health-driven imperative of avoiding 'bed-blocking'. People whose discharge from hospital depended on a service being in place tended to access an assessment, whatever their risk rating.

Therefore, in all but the specialist teams, access to assessment tended to be denied to:

- people who were disabled and had needs but were not deemed to be at risk;
- people whose needs could not obviously be related to a local authority-provided service;
- people with an entitlement to an assessment who failed to satisfy risk-based eligibility criteria.

Level and type of assessment accessed

The linking of eligibility to the predicted requirement for services in the Older Person's, Generic and Hospital Teams meant that most people were seen to require only a 'low-level' assessment, that is, one directed at determining eligibility for a particular type of service. Hence many people accessing an assessment via the Older Person's and Generic Teams received their assessment from the person directly responsible for arranging their services. In the case of the Hospital Team, social workers appeared to act largely as proxy home care supervisors.

In both these types of team assessments were predominantly service-led. Unmet need was rarely recorded, and any requirement for services not available through the department tended to go unacknowledged. Except in the case of older people, however, the specialist teams offered a 'full' assessment to all comers, although this could entail a considerable wait. Risk-based eligibility criteria were used less to keep people out, or to test their eligibility for differing types and levels of assessment, than to hold them in line for a needs-based assessment.

This variation in practice is obviously shaped by differential levels of demand. It may also relate the age group served by the different types of team. Given the long-standing tendency among social workers to see older people as requiring mostly 'practical' assistance rather than specialist social work skills, the service-led approach of the Older Person's, Generic and Hospital Teams was doubtless reinforced by the predominantly elderly constituency of these teams.

The accessibility of assessment

Social workers on the Older Person's and Generic Teams used eligibility criteria and means-testing as a means of limiting access to a 'full' assessment and care management to all but a minority of applicants. Hospital social workers also used eligibility criteria strategically, as a means of accessing people to a sufficient level of services to expedite their discharge. People assessed by these two types of team were systematically marginalised by the reliance of social workers on other professionals or carers to reach a decision about eligibility. Indeed, many people were quite likely to be unaware they had had an assessment at all.

In the Older Person's and Generic Teams an awareness of the mismatch between limited resources and tightening budgets on the one hand and pent-up demand on the other fed through into front-line practice. People applying for assistance were liable to construction as 'demanding' and a potentially dangerous drain on resources.

The specialist teams, however, were less dependent on services provided or funded by the local authorities concerned. The waiting list system also afforded social workers more time to devote to each assessment. These teams therefore saw the issue of access in terms making the process of assessment accessible and helping people gain access to services. Staff were more open about service deficiencies and gaps and would attempt to mould existing services to individual needs.

The Hospital Team was in the same authority as the Younger Person's Team and social workers on both teams shared a commitment to advocacy. On occasion, therefore, if patients were constructed as social services department clients who required defending against health service management, the hospital social workers would see their role as to advocate on behalf of these citizens.

The role of carers

Social workers tended to position carers differently in assessment according to the type of team on which they were working. All, however, had a tendency to treat 'users' and 'carers' as separate units of assessment rather than an inter-related whole. This in turn could serve to create or exaggerate conflicts of interest between those concerned.

Except where an older person was involved, social workers on the specialist teams tended to place the disabled person at the centre of their assessments. This could serve to marginalise carers' needs and interests and exacerbate family tensions. On the Older Person's and Generic Teams, the importance of sustaining carers in their role more frequently led to their needs being prioritised in assessment.

Social workers on the Hospital Team might, on occasion, step in to advocate on behalf of the disabled person. Generally, though, carers were an essential component of a speedy discharge and, as such, dominated the assessment process. This could of course act against carers' interests, drawing them unwillingly into 'packages of care'.

The next chapter will consider in greater detail what the assessment process looks like from the perspective of disabled people and their carers.

3

The perspectives of disabled people and carers

This chapter considers access to assessment from the perspectives of disabled people and carers. It draws on interviews with 50 disabled people and 23 carers who had had some assessment contact with social workers from the two local authorities (see Appendix A for details), as well as observations of assessment practice in the six social work teams. The chapter begins by discussing how assessment was understood by the disabled people and carers interviewed; it goes on to explore the concerns which they identified about accessing assessment.

Understanding assessment

The disabled people and carers interviewed in this study were asked how and why they tried to access assessment, what happened as a result and what they thought of the outcomes of their assessment contact with social workers. What emerged from these interviews was that the term 'assessment' meant little to most people.

Assessment as a process which "should take account of the wishes of the individuals and where possible should include their active participation" (Secretaries of State, 1989, para 3.2.6) was not part of the accounts which most people gave of their contacts with social workers. Individuals had a great deal to say about why and how they had tried to make contact with social services departments. They talked at length about their views of the exchanges they had had with social workers and other professionals. Many people also had views about the services they were receiving or not receiving as a result of these contacts. But most people did not understand that these contacts were defined by social workers and their employing organisations as assessments of their needs.

The majority of disabled people and carers interviewed struggled to make sense of what one man called "this social service business". People tended to talk about the encounters they had had with social workers in terms of what was happening in their lives at the time and how social workers had understood or ignored their circumstances. But most people were not aware that they had a right to assessment or that their needs had been considered by a social worker. The lack of awareness which most people had of being a part, active or otherwise, of an assessment process, supports findings from other studies which have sought disabled people and carers' views of community care services (Baldock and Ungerson, 1994). It also raised important questions for local authority social services departments and their staff about the purpose and process of assessment.

A minority of disabled people interviewed were aware that they had accessed assessment. The visually impaired people who had had contact with Authority B knew that their formal registration was also an assessment for services. They were able to talk about the purpose of the contact they had had with practitioners as well as the outcomes. They were aware of the procedures involved. They felt they had had time to prepare themselves for the assessment; before they were visited they had received and become familiar with the information sent to them about registration and assessment.

In addition some people who had had contact with social workers from the younger disabled or Deaf Teams described these as occasions on which they had been asked for their views on their situations, been listened to and become involved in making decisions about how their needs could be met.

But these experiences were the exception. Most people interviewed could not provide a view of accessing assessment which connected with the organisational and professional accounts of the assessment process. Disabled people and carers shared accounts of fragmentary and often confusing and frustrating contacts that had not been experienced as coherently centred on their needs.

What emerged from the interviews was detailed commentary on what led to social work contact, what happened subsequently and whether this helped or hindered the ways in which disabled people and carers were managing their lives. From these accounts six concerns emerged which raise important questions about the experience of assessing assessment:

- initiating contact with social services departments;
- being referred for assessment;
- contacts with social workers;
- the categorisation of carers and users;
- the limits and benefits of assessment;
- definitions of risk.

Initiating contact with social service departments

Disabled people and carers had a number of reasons for contacting social services departments. Some wanted information to assist them in considering options and reaching decisions about what they should do. Some were seeking advice on their situations. Some wanted to enquire about how they could get a specific service. No one interviewed described making initial contact because they required support and assistance and knew that they might be entitled to an assessment of their needs from the local authority. It was either the advice and assistance of informal networks or insider knowledge that was critical to them making an initial contact with local authority social services departments.

Using informal networks

Disabled people and carers often approached their local social services department on the advice of friends, family or acquaintances.

Example 1

Mr L was a 64-year-old man who had spent some time in hospital when a fellow patient suggested that he contact social services.

Mrs L: "While you were in [hospital] there was another chap very similar to you, wasn't there, who suggested that you get in touch with social services because he'd been in touch with them himself, and was having various things to help him."

Mr L: "Well, I didn't know anything at all about this social service business. But he was in the opposite bed and he was in a bad way, very similar to me, but he'd also got emphysema and he couldn't hardly walk at all - but he had to fend for himself at home. He told me he was having a stair rail put in, and he weren't having to pay for it. He was also having a walk-in shower put in which he wasn't having to pay for, and he suggested that I should do the same."

For Mr L it was timely advice from a service user who was reassuring about the financial costs involved which led him to approach a social worker.

Several disabled people said they had relatives, friends or neighbours who were receiving a service that they thought might help them too. They therefore approached their local social services department to ask for that service and as a result were drawn into the assessment process. For others, particularly those in hospital, it was seeing social workers visit other people that prompted them to ask if they could also see one.

Using insider knowledge
Disabled people who already received a service described using insider knowledge of the social services department to access assessment for further support.

Example 2

Mrs W was a 78-year-old woman who had received a home help service for many years. She said she had a phone number that she would ring if she needed extra help in other ways.

Q: "Who is on that number? The social worker?"
Mrs W: "No. Home helps. You see, if you get in touch with the social worker you have to wait for her to come round and see you. If you go to the home helps, they can organise what you need, it is quicker."

Knowing the system, and knowing who to ask for help seemed to work most effectively for people who lived alone and were regarded, by the services, as being at risk. Several carers described situations where their insider knowledge did not accelerate access to assessment. As they became only too aware their presence as carers in a household reduced the priority given by some social workers to the pressing needs of the disabled person they lived with.

Example 3

Mrs R was a 63-year-old woman who cared for her husband who had multiple sclerosis and restricted mobility. She had been having increasing difficulty managing to bathe him and had been trying for months to get help from the social services department. Then she had a heart attack and had to go into hospital. She described the change that this triggered in service response.

Mrs R: "Up until then there was nothing. Until I had the heart attack, and then of course they were all here then, but until then.... I'd rung up to ask about the bath and months and months went by and they didn't even reply or make an appointment.... When it was just to try and get in touch with them for help for [Mr R], it was so long winded and they were so busy, there was only the one man on the area and they couldn't get to you for months and months. But as soon as anything happened to me, and he was left out on a limb on his own, they were there."

Mr and Mrs R's contact was with the Generic Team. Mr R had a legal right to an assessment but was considered to be a low priority case and was not assessed until the loss of his main carer meant that he moved to the high priority category.

Both local authorities in this study produced information about services and assessments in the form of leaflets and booklets. None of the disabled people or carers interviewed in this study who took the initiative in making contact did so as a result of obtaining and reading these leaflets. The one form of written information which was mentioned was the telephone book. But it could not always deliver what was required.

Example 4

Mrs H, a 79-year-old woman, described how an earlier attempt to make contact with social services had come to nothing when she thought she would ring social services to ask for some help, opened the phone book and found that "if you decide to ring social services there are about 100 numbers". She wasn't sure which one to try and was worried about her phone bill mounting up.

These accounts of the ways into accessing assessment which disabled people and carers took raise important practical issues for local authority social services departments as lead agencies for community care to pursue in relation to the dissemination of information about services.

Being referred for assessment

For some disabled people and carers initial contacts with social workers were arranged by others, sometimes without their knowledge. As a result disabled people could find themselves in encounters they had not sought. The two groups in this study who were most likely to have such encounters were people who had been admitted to hospital and people who were being registered blind or partially sighted.

For many of those who had been admitted to hospital it was usual for the initial assessment contacts with social workers to be arranged by hospital nurses (as described in Chapter 2). Disabled people who had been assessed in hospital were often surprised when they were suddenly visited by a social worker and found it difficult to distinguish them from the other professionals they had been seeing. In these situations people often described themselves as feeling too surprised or poorly to say much.

Observations of assessment contacts in hospital indicated that social workers rarely provided disabled people with an explanation of who they were or indicated that the interview that was taking place was an assessment for services. Social workers' prime concern appeared to be to carry out assessments as quickly as possible and explanations about the purpose or assessment procedures were viewed as time consuming.

Some older people who found themselves referred to a hospital social worker refused to have contact with them when they arrived on the ward. These were people who were aware of the service charges which local authority social services departments could make. Despite the judgements of professionals about their need for an assessment these older people refused to speak to a social worker because they thought that contact could result in them having to pay for services that they could not afford. Among this group there were particular fears that a social worker might decide that they needed residential care and as a result they would have to sell their homes.

For some people such fears could be prompted or reinforced by their initial contact with social workers who were alerting people to charging policies on initial contact in order to manage demand for services.

Example 5

Mrs D: "The only thing I didn't like about social services was when [my husband] went in [to hospital] in October when he had his two strokes, the social workers said about him going into a home, which I didn't want him to. The first words she said were 'Do you own this house?' and I said 'Yes.' She said 'Well, you'll have to sell it to have him looked after.' Those were her very words. I said 'Over my dead body will you sell this house while [my husband] and I are alive.'"

Ongoing concerns with the financial consequences of service use were expressed in a number of interviews by carers as well as disabled people. Ms D, whose mother had come to live with her after a spell in hospital, was concerned about the potential threat to her home because of the decision they had made about her mother's care. She used the interview to spell out her position, "Just for the record, this is my home, so it is not (nothing against my mother) but it is not for my mother to be able to sell to pay for everything."

Being registered blind or partially sighted was the other main way in which assessments in this study were set in motion by other people. The Blind Team were responsible for carrying out registrations for everyone in Authority B who was considered to be blind or partially sighted by a consultant. The registration process was used as an assessment process. Because practitioners in the team were committed to working *with* disabled people they took great pains to inform people of the assessment/registration process.

Everyone received a letter prior to their registration, explaining the registration process and letting them know that they would have an assessment visit. People who had experienced this procedures appreciated this approach. There was a high level of understanding of assessment in this group and contact with practitioners was highly valued.

> ## Example 6
> Mr and Mrs I were an older couple who were both assessed through registration as blind.
>
> Mrs I: "We had the people from the Blind Association, the assessors. They said what was needed. The one that came was blind, so of course we didn't have to say what we could and couldn't do, he knew exactly. He said that we could do with a rail somewhere."

These accounts suggest that disabled people who found themselves referred for an assessment were able to use it to share their concerns if they were given information and time to prepare. Without notice the usefulness of such contacts from the perspective of disabled people w limited and frustrating.

Contact with social workers

Disabled people and carers in this study accessed assessment through a range of social work contacts. Some were assessed without seeing or speaking to a social worker. Some had only telephone contacts; others brief face-to-face contacts; some had lengthy or repeated contact. Whatever the type of contact, few people understood that an investigation of their needs was being undertaken.

When Baldock and Ungerson (1994) researched the assessment experiences of 32 stroke victims they noted that people had little awareness of when and how assessment had taken place. The authors suggested that in part "this might have been a reflection of the common problem of forgetfulness in old age" (Baldock and Ungerson, 1994).

In this study observations of a range of assessment encounters by phone or face-to-face indicated that a lack of recall about accessing and receiving an assessment was not just a matter of the forgetfulness of disabled people and carers. It was observed on a regular basis, particularly in the work of the Hospital, Generic and Older Person's Teams, that assessment exchanges often limited disabled people's participation in, as well as understanding of, assessment.

The limited time given to assessment encounters by social workers, particularly in the Hospital, Generic and Older Person's Teams, as well as the lack of information they provided about their role posed a barrier to participation and understanding.

Example 7

Mrs D, who was an 85-year-old woman, was admitted to hospital for a while after her husband died. She decided to go and live with her daughter when she was discharged.

Q: "When you were in hospital, did you talk to a social worker?"
Mrs D: "I think it was a social worker. Well, they asked me what I wanted, what I needed, two ladies. Who did we talk to [daughter]? those two who came to see me?"
Ms D: "Well, we saw physiotherapists, an occupational therapist, who came round last week to do an assessment on mum for a stair lift, and we did speak to a couple of social workers, yes, when we really needed a bath rail. What happens is, they give you their name when they come in, but my mum was so ill that you don't take the name in. What they really ought to do is give you a card with their name on, that would be ever such a help, and then you could know who to refer back to when you've made a request."

If people were left after these brief contacts with further questions to raise or information to provide it was not easy for them to take the initiative in pursuing them. It was not routine for most social workers to leave information with disabled people about who they were and how they could be contacted. People who were not given the name, job title and contact number of the social worker were effectively excluded from participating further in the decisions being made about their needs.

Barriers to communication in assessment encounters arose from the preoccupation of some social workers with the considerable paperwork associated with assessment. Concern with completing items on checklists and forms blunted responsiveness to what disabled people and carers were saying and discouraged disabled people and carers from sharing more information about their situations.

Social workers' use of 'service language' also played a part in limiting exchanges with disabled people and carers. It was often the case that when social workers used terms such as 'personal care needs', 'domiciliary carers' and 'being mobile' and 'self-caring', they did so with no explanation about what these terms meant. As one disabled person observed, the terms used by social workers could be very misleading. She thought that 'personal care' referred to whether she could use her washing machine, and 'being mobile' meant having a car.

Communication difficulties were greater for those disabled people and carers whose first language was not English. Observations of assessment contacts as well as the experiences shared with us by two Guerjarati speaking disabled people and carers indicated that it was unusual for arrangements to be made for interpreters to be present for assessments. Disabled people and carers were left to rely on family members to interpret what was being said. It was often the case that the 'service language' being used by social workers could not be readily understood by these interpreters. As a result considerable limits were placed on the questions asked as well as the information provided to social workers about needs and circumstances.

Example 8

Mr K and Mr M were older men who spoke Guerjarati. When they were assessed in hospital both had had to rely on family members to interpret what the social worker was saying to them. Both said that they had not received much information about assessments. They would have liked to have been given information about services that they could have taken away with them, but they had not wanted to ask about this through family members.

The methods of assessment used by social workers could also pose barriers for disabled people. Some of the disabled people who were assessed by practitioners in the Generic and Older Person's Teams had difficulties with telephone assessments.

Example 9

Mr C was an older man, who avoided long phone conversations because of his breathlessness. He described what happened when he phoned the generic team.

Mr C: "When I eventually came out of hospital I rang the social services and she asked me what I wanted - on the phone, actually. I was a little bit put out, I must admit. She was a nice girl, I met her afterwards, but she said what do you want?, and I said I didn't know what I wanted. And she tried to talk to me on the phone, and I thought that was impossible. I said I can't talk to you on the phone, I can't tell you what I want. I said I want you to tell me what I'm entitled to and what I'm not entitled to. In other words, tell me all about it because I just don't know."

Mr C challenged the Generic Team's routine method of assessment (see Chapter 2). His challenge succeeded in getting him a face-to-face encounter that he used to explore his options.

For a number of people contact with a social worker was followed by a long delay in hearing anything. For people new to social services this could be a source of worry and frustration. For some people who were experienced service users these delays confirmed their concerns about the diminishing resources that were available to them.

Example 10

Mrs C lived with her son, who was a long term service user with learning difficulties and known to the Deaf Team. When she was interviewed in March she had been trying to access an assessment for him for funding a short stay in a residential home.

Mrs C: "The system takes an awfully long time now to get anything done. I asked for a meeting in January and it still hasn't been sorted out yet, and I think that is a long time to be waiting. Had I been desperate, had I got a difficult son, I could be tearing my hair out now."

Q: "When you say you asked for a meeting, was that with a social worker?"
Mrs C: "I asked for a meeting with the social worker in January and I
actually met him - I phoned for an appointment on the 10th of January, I
had a letter for him to come, and he actually arrived here the beginning
of March. I was really annoyed that I had to wait so long. He came back
to me the following week to go through all the papers and all the
formalities, so that is two weeks ago. And I still haven't heard whether
I've got funding or not."

The delay in this assessment had been partly due to the illness of a staff
member. Mrs C had a lot of experience of social services and she was
very concerned about staffing:

Mrs C: "We haven't got a full-time member of staff in the social services
team for Deaf people, other than [social worker].... It would be a great
improvement to have at least one other member, if not two full-time
members of staff that we know are going to be there, that can come and
visit or answer our questions. Over this episode I've rung up several times
and there hasn't been a member of staff even on duty."

What emerged from these accounts was a picture of the work which
disabled people and carers do in trying to make sense of their contacts
with social workers. This work was rarely described as a joint enterprise
or partnership to achieve an agreed outcome. Rather it was directed at
trying to stitch together fragments of contact and connect them to
people's most pressing concerns.

Categorising carers and users

A recurring issue in people's accounts of assessment contacts was the
way in which social workers and their organisations categorised people
as either users or carers. From the perspective of disabled people and
carers this practice took little account of the fact that many disabled
people were caring for others and the patterns of caring relationships in
many households were complex and changing.

Example 11

Mrs Q was a 72-year-old woman who had received an assessment of her needs in hospital while she was recovering from a heart attack. She cared for her husband, who had had a stroke and lost the use of most of his right side. Mr Q cared for her when she returned from hospital. They jointly cared for their son, who had epilepsy and schizophrenia, and he cared for both of them, depending on how well he was feeling.

Disabled people and carers recognised that social workers and their organisations often had problems grasping these realities. The response that was made to the situation in the Q household was to adopt the standard practice in the Hospital Team when a request for help with housework was made. Mrs Q was given a list of private housework agencies so that she could organise any help with housework she needed.

Some people discovered that if the caring work undertaken in a household did not 'fit' the assessment pro forma used by the social worker there could be delays and considerable difficulties for disabled people in accessing a full assessment for services while social workers negotiated whose responsibility it was and whose budget would cover any costs that resulted.

Example 12

Mrs P was caring for her husband, who had contact with the specialist sensory impairment team. She went into hospital for a hip replacement operation, and needed an assessment. But it was not clear to the social workers involved who should carry out the assessment. Was she her husband's carer? (in which case her assessment should be carried out by her husband's team), or was she a new referral? During the observation period of this study, at least three different team managers were arguing over which team was responsible for assessing Mrs P's needs. Eventually the Younger Person's Team carried out her assessment, designating Mrs P's husband as her main carer.

Another issue raised by disabled people who had children was the way in which their caring responsibilities as parents seemed difficult for social workers to respond to because of the manner in which carers and users were categorised and their needs assessed.

Example 13

Mrs A was a 50-year old Irish woman. She had a bone marrow disease and needed frequent blood transfusions, which left her feeling very ill and weak. She found caring for her two children very difficult when she returned from her blood transfusions, and while in hospital she asked a social worker for some help.

Mrs A: "I was quite ill. I live with my two children, and it is enough to cope with them when you're feeling well. So I asked social services to get me some help. Because I could make a cup of tea myself and look after myself, they said 'oh no, we can't do anything for you'."

Q: "Did you contact a social worker while you were in hospital?"

Mrs A: "Yes, I did. The nurse said to me, when you go home, you shouldn't jump into work and that, you won't be able to do it, and I thought, well, who else is going to do it? You can't expect the kids to be adults, because they're not adults, they're kids. That was the idea, that maybe they could find some way of helping me, but they couldn't. I didn't meet their criteria, because I could make a cup of tea and I could get the dinner on, and I could get dressed myself, so I didn't qualify."

The only suggestion made by the social worker was foster care for her children. Mrs A didn't want that, as she explained:

Mrs A: "I didn't think it would work for the kids, I didn't want to take them out of the house. There is enough upheaval in their lives as it is.

The difficulties Mrs A faced in managing were substantial. She was clear about the kind of assistance that would enable her to cope and her view was shared by an involved health professional. But the basis on which the local authority social services department was categorising carers and users in its assessment for community care services meant that the only response they could offer was, in Mrs A's view, inappropriate.

The categorisation of users and carers required by the managerial and financial arrangements of social services departments placed real limits on the way in which workers and disabled people and carers could work with the complex and changing realities of care and service use. For those at the receiving end the consequences could add to the considerable difficulties already being managed.

The limits and benefits of assessment

From the viewpoint of disabled people the limits on assessment were not just confined to issues of care, service use and budgets. They found the framework used for assessment work was too narrow to encompass the range of their needs.

Many disabled people faced considerable financial difficulties. They were worried about how to pay for food, heating and rent, as well as covering the extra costs of disability. Although some disabled people received help from social workers with applying for social security benefits such responses were not standard practice. Most social workers did not consider debt or benefit advice to be part of assessment work. As a result they either disregarded financial problems or they would suggest that people contact other agencies such as the Benefits Agency or Citizens Advice Bureau. Other social workers did offer financial advice and help. But most were not comfortable working in this area despite the fact that maximising benefit income was considered increasingly important by their organisations to raise revenue through service charges.

Housing was another major concern for disabled people and carers. Many people described struggling because of poor standards of accommodation and inaccessible housing. Some social workers, usually those in the specialist teams, responded to these concerns by referring disabled people on to occupational therapists, or by supporting applications for sheltered housing. But most did not appear to consider housing needs as part of their assessment work.

Increasing impairment was associated with increasing social isolation for many people in this study. Loss of the ability to drive, garden, or walk to friends' houses often left people isolated and lonely. Social workers' responses to these expressed needs were reported by disabled people as being service-limited with little discussion of alternatives. As one woman expressed it, "sitting around with a lot of other old women who I don't know would not restore my sense of being included in the community."

Many carers also found that they were experiencing increasing social isolation. They could not visit friends or relatives if it meant leaving a disabled person alone, and sometimes trips together to visit friends turned out to be more bother than they were worth. Carers particularly missed holidays but it was rare for social workers to discuss this or put people in touch with relevant organisations.

Disabled people and carers found the limits of assessment frustrating when their request for a specific service to meet their needs were refused by a social worker. Sometimes people were told that there were no resources. When they received no explanation people tended to think that the social worker had decided that their need was not important enough to be taken into account.

For some people the response of the social worker seemed a combination of both.

Example 14

Mrs P was a 65-year-old South Asian woman whose husband had had a stroke and she was finding it difficult to help him to the toilet and bath him.

Mrs P: "I contacted the social worker for a commode, but they refused to give that to him. They say he doesn't need it but I think he does. I don't really need anything else apart from the commode. In the night, when he gets up to go to the loo, I have to take him in the wheelchair. We were offered a commode without wheels, but that is no good to him because he can't walk. Social services told us we had to buy one - but the hospital told us to ask the social services for one. I have also asked the social worker for a shower to be fitted because I couldn't manage to give him a bath."

Q: "Are you still finding it very difficult to bath Mr P?"

Mrs P: "The social services gave us a chair which fits into the bath, so I manage to give him a bath that way, it is a bit easier, but we really need a shower. I applied for a shower in July but we've been told we can't have anything at the moment because of a lack of money. But I am strong."

Most people interviewed were aware that local authorities were working with very limited resources. When this resulted in them being assessed as needing a service and then not receiving it responses were mixed. Some people felt angry but powerless and lived with the decision that their needs were not considered urgent, drawing on their strengths, like Mrs P, to carry on. Others tried to publicise their situation in an attempt to get the urgency of their needs reconsidered.

Example 15

Mrs Y had been promised a shower, then was told she would have to wait until April because the funds had run out. When Mrs Y enquired in April, she was told she had to wait a further 12 months because there was still no money in the budget. She described the phone conversation:

Mrs Y: "I said, 'how very fortunate, because I've got a mental health nurse coming in tomorrow morning, and I've also got a researcher from Birmingham University in the afternoon, and I'll be able to tell them about this'. And she said, 'oh, researching about what?' And I said, 'well, the treatment that disabled people received from their local community'. 'Oh', she said, 'I'll get the manager to give you a ring'. He didn't ring until the afternoon. He said, 'You'll never believe this, but I thought there was no money in the kitty, and I've just had this list given to me and you're at the top of the emergency list to have your new shower'. I said, 'You're quite right, isn't it a coincidence? A few hours ago I was told no chance, no chance at all, and as soon as I tell them you're come today and I shall tell you my difficulties, suddenly, miraculously, they've found the money to do it!' I'm very grateful for that, maybe the same people that are funding your research are funding my shower!"

Other disabled people and their carers described threatening to involve local councillors, or the local press, to get services or equipment that they had been promised by social workers. Only three people interviewed had taken the step of formally complaining to the social work team involved. The rest had decided to wait and manage as best they could.

Not everyone who was interviewed focused on the limits of assessment. Some people talked about how assessment had extended the options which were available to them in managing their lives. All these were people who had had contact with the Younger Disabled, Deaf and Blind Teams. In these accounts social workers who took time to understand people's circumstances and needs and were there when crises occurred were particularly valued. Relationships which had been built with social workers over time were also valued.

Example 16

Mr O was a 55-year-old Irish man. He had multiple sclerosis, and had known his social worker, who was a disabled person, from the Younger Person's Team for about three years. He explained why that was an advantage:

Mr O: "She knows my circumstances, because when I was in the nursing home she got to know me quite well. I was going through a lot - that was the worst part of my life. My wife was divorcing me at the time, and she had put me in the nursing home. It was such a traumatic couple of years that [social worker] became quite involved with that side of things."

Mr O had moved back home with the support of the social worker. Mr O decided he wanted to remain there for as long as possible. In working with him to meet his increasing need for personal care and assistance the social worker had looked outside the local authority services and suggested that Mr O made an application to the Independent Living Fund for extra money to provide 24-hour care. Mr O had discussed this application thoroughly before he decided to go ahead. When asked what he thought about this proposed change in his situation replied:

Mr O: "I'm quite keen on it actually. I know a woman, she's got MS and she has 24-hour care. Her daughter says that since her mum has had the 24-hour care, her mum is got more of a social life than she has! Because they take you out, they take you shopping, take you to the pictures, put you to bed at the time you want to go to bed."

The social worker had Mr O's trust and was working to support his wishes without being limited by the services available through the local authority. Her approach contrasted strongly with the views expressed by many of the social workers in the Generic and Older Person's Teams that 24-hour home-based care made individuals 'too dependent' on services.

Definitions of risk

As Chapter 2 indicated risk plays an important part in the way in which social workers and social services departments target assessments and services. Risk was also an issue which disabled people and carers raised when talking about their needs and concerns.

Disabled people and carers suggested that their concerns about risk were variably addressed by social workers. In part this variation reflected differences between the disabled person's perception of risk and that of the social worker. It could also reflect differences between a disabled person and a carer's perception of risk and the way in which social workers responded to these differences.

One of the greatest concerns to disabled people (particularly older and blind people) was their risk of falling or burning themselves. For some, this meant that they only felt safe in their own home. As Mrs I, a 73-year-old woman, who was blind, explained:

> "I know how to feel my way about, and I know how to feel my way upstairs with my foot. In this house I can go anywhere. I know how many steps to the door, know exactly where to go, know where every piece of furniture is. If things are changed around I'd have a hell of a job, but as long as everything is left in place I can suss my way around. If I go to somewhere strange or other people is houses, then I can't ... this is the only place I feel safe."

Practitioners in the Blind Team were often valued because of their direct and practical responses to reducing the risks faced by people. They accessed long cane training, guide dogs and kitchen training for people to help them with risk reduction.

Some disabled people, like Mr O (above) also expressed appreciation at the way in which social workers supported them, rather than their relatives, in their decision to take risks such as remaining in their own homes despite the wishes of others. But others, like Mr B (see Chapter 2) felt thwarted when social workers disagreed with them over what was an acceptable level of risk and involved other people against their wishes.

Carers also described conflicts with social workers over what level of risk it was acceptable for disabled people to take. Sometimes this conflict centred on the views each party held of the role that carers could play in reducing the risks faced by the disabled person. In cases of conflict between disabled people and carers over risk, disabled people could find the social worker agreeing with carers. The assessment which resulted would meet the carer's concerns about the disabled person's risk, rather than meeting the disabled person's wishes.

However, as a number of people commented, there were some risks that they considered were associated with service delivery that social workers seemed to disregard altogether. Older people often expressed a view that it was risky to allow strangers into their home. They were unhappy about letting the social worker in, or agreeing to paid carers coming in, because they feared burglary or attack. Participating in an assessment which led to the delivery of such services was seen by some disabled people as increasing the risks they faced in their daily lives but they did not consider that social workers took their views of such risk seriously.

For others it was the failure of an assessment response at times of vulnerability that was seen to increase the risks they faced.

Example 17

Mrs D an older woman had received treatment in a private hospital and needed assistance at home following her discharge.

Mrs D: "To me the only downfall of the whole issue was the fact that I was out of hospital for eight days before I got any help, and that is when I wanted it. They phoned from [private hospital] to [local social services] as I came home on the Monday. Now, I would have thought somewhere along the line they could have arranged with somebody that I got help that Monday evening. Because when I got home on the Monday, they told me to phone straightaway, which I did. 'Oh well', they said 'we'll send somebody out to assess you (this is from [local social services]) we don't know what you want' and it was all passing the buck from one to another. I was in desperation, because I had that bout of diarrhoea. Luckily my granddaughter came and she said 'I'll stay with you grandma'. It was the school holidays, and if I hadn't had her I honestly do not know how I would have coped. I couldn't have done it."

Conclusions

Accessing assessment, from the viewpoint of most of the disabled people and carers interviewed, was an experience of uncertainty, confusion, marginalisation and exclusion. It is not a process which often involved disabled people in active participation in review and decision making. For a small number of people assessment had been well understood and was highly valued. These people had had contact with social work teams that had adopted practices which were informed by a commitment to partnership with disabled people.

The main concerns raised by disabled people and carers in relation to assessment were about the problems they experienced when negotiating with assessment procedures and processes. These problems were related to contacts with organisations and their staff as well as the way in which organisations and their staff delivered assessment. Disabled people and carers shared experiences that highlighted the negative impact assessment encounters can have on their lives. Yet there was also some evidence that more open assessment practice can usefully extend the resources available to disabled people and carers.

Important differences were highlighted in these interviews between the ways in which social workers and local authority social services departments are categorising users and carers and the ways in which disabled people experience caring in their lives. These differences appear to pose real barriers for some disabled people and carers accessing advice and assistance about how to maintain themselves independently at home.

Diversity and difference was noted in the way in which disabled people and carers define risk and the more limited understanding of risk used by social workers and their organisations. Risks associated by disabled people with service delivery were routinely discounted by most social workers. The ways in which social workers responded to differences in the perception of risk which existed between some disabled people and carers also raised questions about whose interests assessment was serving.

The perspectives on accessing assessment which disabled people and carers have to offer are critical to considering the outcomes of current assessment policy and procedure. The assessment practice of social

71

workers, shaped as it is by organisational priorities and imperatives, plays a key role in delivering these outcomes (Morris, 1997). The question which this raises is can this practice change? The next chapter considers what practical lessons can be learnt from the experiences of disabled people and carers.

4

Access to assessment-delivering outcomes

Our interest as researchers was to consider what assessment has to contribute to supporting disabled people to live full and independent lives. This interest alerted us to the ways in which disabled people might be involved or excluded from assessment processes and procedures which identified their 'problem', its solution and the delivery of that solution. Our view is that to realise its potential, assessment has to draw directly on the expertise and experience of disabled people as well as carers.

Much of the assessment practice of social workers which was observed in this study was based on what Smale et al (1993) describe as the 'Procedural model'.

> In this the goal of assessment is to gather information to see if the client 'fits' or meets, certain criteria that will 'make them eligible for services'. Those defining the criteria for eligibility, in effect pre-allocating services for generally identified need, make the judgement as to what sort of person should get what resources. The worker's task is to identify the specific people who match the appropriate degree of need defined within the categories of service available and to exclude those not eligible. (Smale et al, 1993, p 19).

The application of this model meant that in some situations social workers were limiting access to assessment at the earliest possible stage as well as working to limit or eliminate direct contact with disabled people and carers during the assessment process. In both authorities this approach was supported organisationally and managerially as well as being influenced by the way in which social workers were required to input assessment data.

Not all assessment practice which was observed and reported was bound by the procedural model. Some social work teams were 'opening up' access to assessment in ways which shared purpose, acknowledged the legal rights of individuals and moved beyond service-led agendas to identify and use community-based networks and resources. The social workers in these teams were being supported by their organisations and managers to contribute to the development of community-wide networks and resources. Many of them worked with an explicit recognition of the rights of disabled people and the discrimination they faced. It was in these teams that disabled people were employed as social workers.

This study suggests that disabled people and carers found contacts based on the procedural model unhelpful. Most of the disabled people and carers interviewed in this study described encounters with local authority social service departments as confusing, fragmentary and often irrelevant to their concerns and priorities. The study highlighted how little most disabled people and carers had understood about the purpose of the assessment encounters they had found themselves in.

The accounts provided by disabled people and carers suggested that they experienced a fundamental lack of connection between assessment and the ways in which they were working out how to manage and resource their changing situations. At times social workers appeared disinterested and unconcerned about the major problems and as a result accessing assessment could add to the pressures and difficulties that disabled people were managing.

The most positive accounts that disabled people and carers gave of assessment encounters were related to assessment practice that provided information about purpose, included face-to-face encounters which focused on people's definitions of their main concerns and valued them and their expertise. Such an approach could not surmount the limited local authority resources available but it could creatively open up alternative ways of managing things. As we have noted our study indicated such encounters were more likely to be experienced by younger disabled people than older people. There was evidence that this differential response was connected to the way in which entitlement to access assessment was understood and applied by social workers and their organisations.

The practical lessons which can be drawn from this study apply across the range of assessment practice that has been identified. They have a relevance to the changing statutory and financial frameworks in which community care services are being delivered (SSI, 1991). They are lessons that can be used to inform the review, development and evaluation of assessment outcomes at practice and policy levels. They can also play a part in the work which disabled people, carers and their organisations are undertaking with local authorities as lead agencies in community care.

Advice and information

Disabled people who require support and assistance in their daily lives are seeking advice and information which will enable them to consider options and reach decisions about what they might do. Local authority social service departments are not providing an accessible advice and information service. Front-line staff are responding to requests for advice and information as potential demands on their services. This response reflects service preoccupations with eligibility and the establishment of risk rather than disabled people's and carers' needs.

As lead agencies for community care social service departments must consider the part they might play in establishing local advice and information services. Such services should be designed to inform, advise and enable. They should cover the full range of available local service providers as well as the issues which are central to disabled people's well-being - income, housing, transport, social and healthcare, employment, training and leisure. Disabled people, carers and their organisations need to work with local authorities to develop these vital services and organisations of disabled and older people must be considered as providers of such services

Communication

Disabled people and carers are facing considerable barriers to accessing and participating in assessments. Some of these arise from the way in which staff and managers of social service organisations communicate with disabled people and carers. Practitioners managing the pressures and tensions of front-line assessment can defensively resort to 'service speak' and jargon. Training and support is essential if such practice is to be challenged and changed.

Practitioners and managers need to acknowledge the importance of communicating clearly and accurately as well as listening to disabled people and carers. Some communication problems reflect a failure to organise and secure the resources required to ensure that people who do not use or understand spoken English easily are not excluded from accessing and participating in assessments. The design of organisational procedures, pro forma and written information also need to be informed by these concerns (SSI, 1991).

Equal access

Disabled people and carers are not accessing assessment equally. There are a number of entry points to assessment which are not always formally recognised within organisations. The statutory entitlement of people to access assessment is not well understood by social workers, social service managers and disabled people. It is a matter of considerable concern that older people appear to be more unequally accessed than others to assessment and services. Some of these issues can be addressed by local authorities making information and advice available. But this is also a matter of training, review and audit. The way in which assessment is delivered needs to be continuously and actively informed by the equality commitments of local authorities social services departments.

Service charges also need to be considered on an equal access agenda (Chetwynd et al, 1996). To meet the concerns raised by disabled people and carers local authority social services departments need to ensure that:

- access to accurate information about charging is available to disabled people who want to make informed choices about service options;
- local authority social services departments decisions about charging policies are informed by disabled people's and carers' views and experiences;
- the procedures devised for charging for services are informed by disabled people's and carers' views and experiences;
- staff are trained and supported to deliver information about service charges in a way that does not operate to restrict access to assessment.

The employment of disabled workers

The expertise which disabled people bring to agencies engaged in assessment is not just in their role as users and/or carers. They also have a part to play as employees. The under-representation of disabled people as social workers, as well as in management positions, needs to be addressed through education, professional training and the recruitment policies of local authorities and voluntary organisations.

What this study revealed is how rarely assessment practice, procedure and policy is building on the frameworks and strategies which disabled people and carers have fashioned to manage their lives. Taking these practical lessons seriously could enable practitioners, managers and policy makers to work more collaboratively and creatively to secure the opportunities which disabled people need to live full and independent lives.

References

Ahmad, W. and Atkin, K. (eds) (1996) *'Race' and community care*, Buckingham: Open University Press.

Audit Commission (1992a) *The community revolution: the personal social services and community care*, London: HMSO.

Audit Commission (1992b) *Community care: managing the cascade of change*, London: HMSO.

Baldock, J. and Ungerson, C. (1994) *Becoming consumers of care: households within the mixed economy of care*, York: Joseph Rowntree Foundation.

Baldwin, S. and Lunt, N. (1996) *Charging ahead, local authority charging policies for community care*, Bristol: The Policy Press.

Butt, J. and Mirza, K. (1996) *Social care and black communities*, London: HMSO.

Cheetham, J. (1993) 'Social work and community care in the 1990s: pitfalls and potentials', in R. Page and J. Baldock (eds) *Social policy review 5*, pp 155-76, London: Social Policy Association.

Chetwynd, M., Ritchie, J., Reith, L. and Howard, M. (1996) *The cost of care: the impact of charging policy on the lives of disabled people*, Bristol: The Policy Press.

Department of Health (1990) *Community care in the next decade and beyond: policy guidance* London: HMSO.

Department of Health, Social Services Inspectorate and Scottish Office Social Work Services Group (1991a) *Care management and assessment: practitioners' guide*, London: HMSO.

Department of Health, Social Services Inspectorate and Scottish Office Social Work Services Group (1991b) *Care management and assessment: managers' guide*, London: HMSO.

Ellis, K. (1993a) *Squaring the circle: user and carer participation in needs assessment*, York: Joseph Rowntree Foundation.

Ellis, K. (1993b) *Analysis of local authority arrangement for care management and assessment published in 1993/4 community care plans*, unpublished.

Gray, A. and Jenkins, B. (1993) 'Markets, managers and the public service: the changing face of a culture', in P. Taylor-Gooby and R. Lawson (eds) *Markets and managers: new issues in the delivery of welfare*, London: Open University Press.

Keep, J. and Clarkson, J. (1996) *Disabled people have rights*, London: RADAR.

Lewis, J. and Glennerster, H. (1996) *Implementing the new community care*, Buckingham: Open University Press.

Morris, J. (1993) *Independent lives? Community care and disabled people*, Basingstoke: Macmillan.

Morris, J. (1997) *Community care: working in partnership with service users*, Birmingham: Venture Press.

Newman, J. and Clarke, J. (1994) 'Going about our business? The managerialization of public services', in J. Clarke, A. Cochrane and E. McLaughlin (eds) *Managing social policy*, London: Sage.

Oliver, M. (1983) *Social work with disabled people*, Basingstoke: Macmillan.

Parrott, D. (1990) *Into the future: a study of the implementation of the Disabled Persons (Services, Consultation and Representation)* Act, 1986, London: RADAR and the London Boroughs Disability Resource Team.

Rummery, K. and Davis, A. (1998) *Community care assessments: what they are and how to get one*, Birmingham: Birmingham Disability Resource Centre and The University of Birmingham.

Secretaries of State for Health, Social Security, Wales and Scotland (1989) *Caring for people. Community care in the next decade and beyond,* Cm 849, London: HMSO.

Smale, G., Tvson, G. (with Brehal, N. and Marsh, P.) (1993) *Empowerment, assessment, care management and the skilled worker,* London: National Institute of Social Work.

Social Services Inspectorate (1991) *Getting the message across: a guide to developing and communicating policies, principle and procedures on assessment,* London: HMSO.

Stevenson, O. and Parsloe, P. (1993) *Community care and empowerment,* York: Joseph Rowntree Foundation.

Twigg, J. and Atkin, K. (1994) *Carers perceived,* Buckingham, Open University Press.

R v Gloucestershire County Council and the Secretary of State ex parte Barry (1997) House of Lords, 20 March, HL *ref.*

(1990) National Health Service and Community Care Act, London: HMSO.

Appendix A: Research methodology

The local authorities
Characteristics
Two local authorities took part in this study. Local Authority A was a metropolitan city council with a predominantly urban population. 9.7% of residents were from minority ethnic communities. Local Authority B was a large county council with a mixture of an urban and rural population. 3.4% of residents were from minority ethnic communities.

Observing assessment procedures
Observations of assessment practice were carried out in the following locations:

- a hospital social work team in Local Authority A ('The Hospital Team');
- a specialist younger disabled person's community social work team in Local Authority A ('The Younger Person's Team');
- a generic community social work team in Local Authority B ('The Generic Team');
- a voluntary organisation for blind and partially sighted people who had contracted the registration and assessment process from Local Authority B ('The Blind Team');
- an older person's community social work team in Local Authority A ('The Older Person's Team');
- a specialist community social work team in Local Authority B offering services to Deaf people ('The Deaf Team').

The researchers' observation notes were written up after each observation day. The teams were offered feedback sessions to check the validity of the data gathered. The results of these feedback sessions were written up as part of the research data. In addition, contact was made with key informants in both local authorities, and policy and practice documentation related to assessment from each team was analysed.

Disabled people and their carers
The sample
A total of 50 disabled people who had been assessed in the time period spanning one month either side of the observation period, and 23 carers who had a relationship with at least one disabled person, were interviewed. Forty disabled people were drawn from local authority

records. Fifteen disabled people were drawn from the records of the Hospital Team, six from the Younger Person's Team, nine from the Generic Team, seven from the Blind Team and three from the Deaf Team. Twenty-one carers associated with this group were interviewed. Ten disabled people and two carers were drawn from other sources, including local disability organisations and carer groups.

The sample was structured to reflect the age profile of disabled people nationally - two thirds of the sample of disabled people were over 65 years old. An attempt was made to ensure that the sample reflected the minority ethnic profile of the populations served by the two local authorities. This had only partial success because of the low numbers of black and Asian people being referred to and accessing social services.

The in-depth interviews

Everyone who had received an assessment during the period of the study in the Hospital Team, Generic Team, Deaf Team and Blind Team was written to and invited to taking part in a semi-structured interview. The Younger Person's Team only permitted the researcher to write to people whose assessments she had observed. The Older Person's Team declined to take part in drawing the interview sample.

Those disabled people who wanted to take part wrote to the researcher and a convenient time and location for the interview was agreed over the phone. Disabled people and carers were given the choice of whether they were interviewed together or separately - they all chose to be interviewed together.

Interviews with Deaf people and non-English speaking people took place with the help of interpreters.

All the interviews were tape-recorded and transcribed. Everyone who took part was given the option of receiving a copy of the transcript of their interview and commenting on it.

Data gathered from all the above source was analysed and has been used in this report.

**DEPARTMENT OF APPLIED
SOCIAL STUDIES AND
SOCIAL RESEARCH**
BARNETT HOUSE
WELLINGTON SQUARE
OXFORD OX1 2ER